IRAN VIOLATIONS OF HUMAN RIGHTS

DOCUMENTS SENT BY AMNESTY INTERNATIONAL TO THE GOVERNMENT OF THE ISLAMIC REPUBLIC OF IRAN

Amnesty International Publications

First published 1987 by Amnesty International Publications
1 Easton Street, London WC1X 8DJ, United Kingdom

Copyright Amnesty International Publications 1987

ISBN 0 86210 123 9
AI Index: MDE 13/09/87
Original Language: English

Printed in England by Shadowdean Ltd, Mitcham, Surrey

Contents

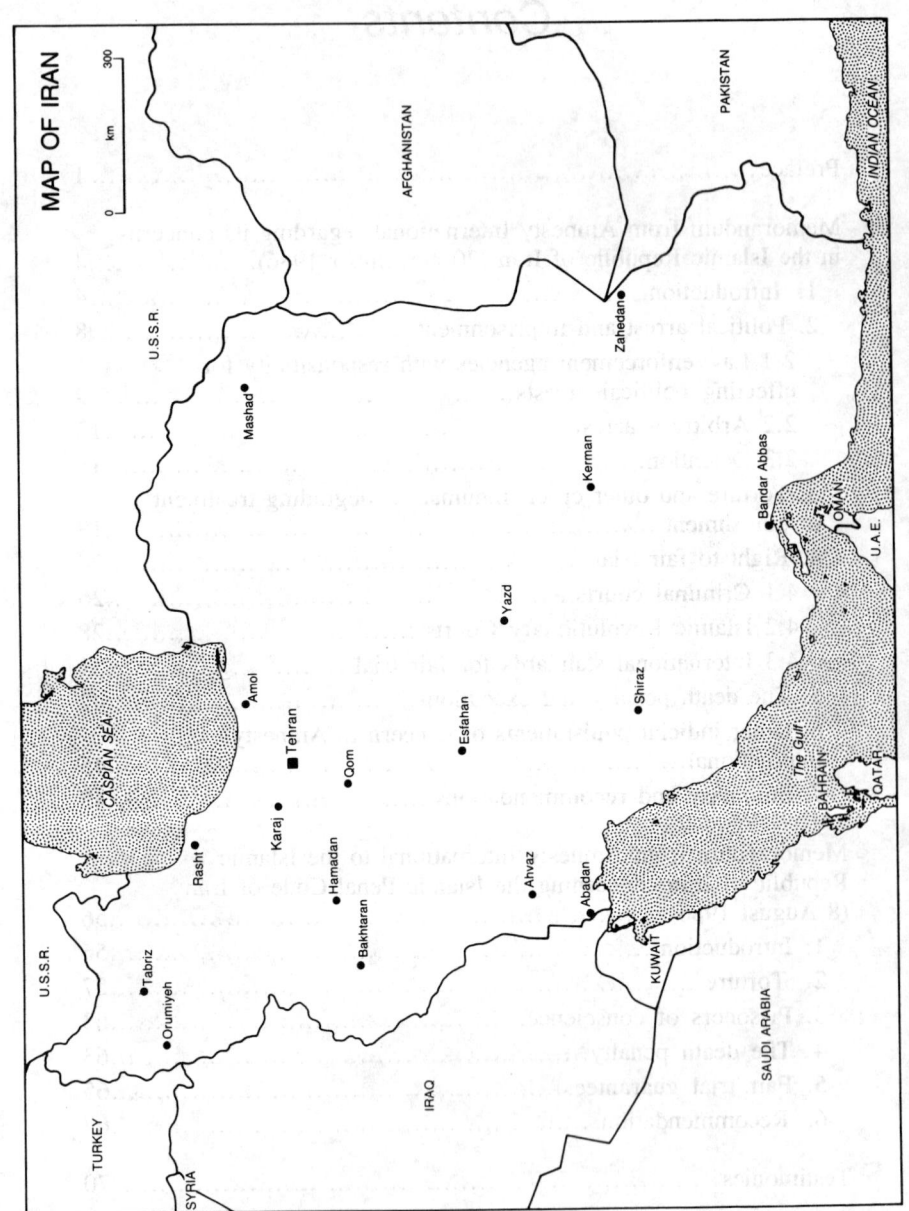

MAP OF IRAN

Preface

The Islamic Republic of Iran was established in 1979, and has been at war with Iraq since 1980. In the eight years that have passed since the February 1979 revolution the country has experienced dramatic and wide-ranging changes affecting all aspects of life. Amnesty International believes that in exceptional circumstances such as these it is all the more important to safeguard fundamental human rights, and that, whatever their nature, such circumstances can never justify the abuse of such rights.

Amnesty International regrets that domestic organizations and associations formed in the late 1970s to monitor and intervene in human rights issues were all forcibly closed down in the early 1980s, as was the Bar Association and its committee on human rights. It also regrets that many of those who worked to uphold and defend the rights of others were themselves imprisoned, executed or forced into exile.

The United Nations (UN) General Assembly has repeatedly drawn attention in resolutions to violations of human rights in the Islamic Republic of Iran, and the UN Commission on Human Rights has appointed a Special Representative to investigate the human rights situation. He, however, has been denied access to the country. Access has also been denied to Amnesty International despite repeated requests.

Amnesty International has continued to work for the victims of human rights violations in Iran as it did before the creation of the Islamic Republic. This publication is part of the movement's continuing efforts to secure an improvement in the respect for human rights. It comprises three sections: two are the edited texts of memoranda sent by Amnesty International to the Government of the Islamic Republic of Iran; the third is testimony given to Amnesty International representatives by former prisoners of conscience and political prisoners.

The first memorandum, *Memorandum from Amnesty International regarding its concerns in the Islamic Republic of Iran*, was sent to the government in November 1986. It does not claim to give an up-to-date record of human rights violations in Iran, but rather represents a pattern of such violations documented by Amnesty International over several years. It covers the range of Amnesty International's statutory concerns: the imprisonment of prisoners of conscience, their arbitrary arrest and detention, unfair trials in political cases, the use of torture and ill-treatment to extract information, and the use of judicial punishments such as the death penalty and the amputation of fingers which Amnesty International considers constitute forms of torture or cruel, inhuman or degrading punishment[1]. The memorandum acknowledges that improvements have taken place, but concludes with a series of recommendations which Amnesty International believes are the minimum guarantees needed to protect the basic human rights of Iranian citizens.

The second memorandum, *Memorandum from Amnesty International to the Islamic Republic of Iran concerning the Islamic Penal Code of Iran*, was sent to the government in August 1986. The Islamic Penal Code of Iran was adopted for an initial trial period of five years. Amnesty International's memorandum is an attempt to make a positive contribution to discussions or revisions of the penal code before its provisions become final. Amnesty International's analysis of the penal code is based on international human rights and humanitarian law. The organization respects the right of states to formulate legislation in accordance with their own social, cultural, religious or other traditions. However, where such legislation falls short of internationally agreed standards for the protection of human rights, Amnesty International is constrained to point this out, and to propose changes aimed at bringing legislation into line with international standards. Iran is a party to the International Covenant on Civil and Political Rights (ICCPR), ratified by countries with widely varying legal systems.

The final section of this publication consists of first-hand testimonies from former prisoners of conscience and political prisoners. Amnesty International cannot vouch for the authenticity of every detail in these accounts, but presents them as examples of individuals suffering because of their political beliefs or activities. They are representative of many more such testimonies in Amnesty International's possession. Names, precise dates and other details which could identify the individual victims have been omitted or

---

[1]While Amnesty International has received allegations of ill-treatment — particularly psychological — of Iraqi prisoners of war in Iranian territory, this subject is not addressed in this publication because of the lack of detailed and verifiable information.

amended because they fear reprisals against relatives still living in Iran.

Amnesty International addressed its memoranda to the Government of the Islamic Republic of Iran and other appropriate authorities in August and November 1986. It explained that while it had made every effort to ensure the accuracy of its documents, it would welcome clarification of any points where it was felt that this had not been achieved. In addition the organization expressed the hope that the documents could form the basis for discussions with the authorities, and reaffirmed its readiness to send a delegation to Tehran for this purpose. It asked the authorities to respond to this proposal or send written comments on the memoranda by the end of December 1986. Amnesty International received no response by that date, and its subsequent approaches to Iranian officials have satisfied the organization that no such response would be received later. Amnesty International regrets the apparent decision of the Government of the Islamic Republic of Iran not to communicate with it and fears that the denial of access to the country cannot but increase its concern that human rights violations there continue unabated.

Memorandum from Amnesty International regarding its concerns in the Islamic Republic of Iran

(20 November 1986)

1. Introduction

This memorandum was compiled on the basis of documented reports of human rights violations within Amnesty International's mandate in the Islamic Republic of Iran during recent years. Amnesty International works for the unconditional release of men and women imprisoned because of their political, religious or other conscientiously held beliefs or because of their ethnic origin, sex, colour or language, provided that they have neither used nor advocated violence (prisoners of conscience). It works for fair and prompt trials for all political prisoners, and opposes the imposition and infliction of the death penalty, and torture or other cruel, inhuman or degrading treatment or punishment of prisoners. The document focuses on the procedures for arresting and detaining opposition political activists or suspects and others imprisoned for their beliefs and/or activities, their treatment during incarceration and their trials. It also examines the range of offences for which the death penalty and other punishments of concern to Amnesty International are provided. The organization's conclusions on these issues and its related recommendations are set out in Section 7 of this memorandum. While every effort has been made to present accurately the matters outlined above, Amnesty International would welcome clarification and comment from the authorities in the Islamic Republic of Iran to whom this memorandum is addressed, and trusts that it may form the basis for future discussions. This memorandum makes several references to an earlier communication sent to the Islamic Republic of Iran entitled *Memorandum from Amnesty International to the Islamic Republic of Iran concerning the Islamic Penal Code of Iran*, dated 8 August 1986.

Amnesty International's efforts to combat human rights violations in Iran have continued for nearly 20 years, during which time its concerns, while varying in scale, have remained the same: the incarceration of prisoners of conscience, unfair trials of political prisoners, torture and ill-treatment, and executions.

Amnesty International has noted with regret that some former prisoners of conscience held during the 1970s when the late Shah was in power, for whose unconditional release it then worked, now figure among those with responsibility for the incarceration of prisoners of conscience and for other human rights violations in Iran. Others who were imprisoned in the 1970s for the non-violent expression of their conscientiously held beliefs are once more in prison, and many have been executed.

Amnesty International recognizes that countries which have experienced a revolution are often in exceptional circumstances and face exceptional difficulties. However, the organization believes that in such situations it is all the more important to safeguard those basic human rights which it strives to protect, and to make every effort not to repeat whatever human rights abuses were suffered during the period previous to the revolution.

Among the main factors conducive to human rights abuses in post-revolution Iran has been the apparent lack of a centralized authority able to ensure the correct treatment of prisoners and the apparent non-uniform application of the law. Individual judges would appear to have had unbridled powers, local officials have used their position to achieve personal gain or to conduct vendettas, and law enforcement authorities have abused their authority by, for instance, inflicting torture on prisoners in their custody. The lack of centralized authority has been conducive to widespread arbitrary arrest and detention, torture and executions, while at the same time denying victims of human rights violations recourse to impartial tribunals whereby they could challenge their detention and present a defence in the course of a fair and public trial. All too often, following summary trials, death sentences have been imposed and swiftly carried out.

The frequently arbitrary nature of the administration of justice in the Islamic Republic of Iran has permitted, among other things, the summary execution of prisoners previously sentenced to imprisonment without the chance of having further judicial hearings, and has resulted in vastly disparate sentences being handed down in different parts of the country for identical offences.

A number of measures have been introduced by the authorities in attempts to counter these practices, including the establishment of a more centralized authority for judicial affairs and the setting up of a ministry with responsibility for the Islamic Revolutionary Guards Corps (IRGC). Other measures include attempts to standardize the parameters of penalties permitted for certain offences. However, years had elapsed before the introduction of such measures, and since their full effect has yet to be felt Amnesty International believes that many more immediate steps must be taken by the authorities if there is to be an end to human rights violations throughout the country and if Iranian citizens are to enjoy those rights which their government is committed to uphold.

In its attempts to achieve the release of prisoners of conscience, fair trials for all political prisoners and an end to torture and the death penalty throughout the world Amnesty International seeks to document individual cases in as much detail as possible and to verify, by checking with other sources, that the information is correct. Research of this kind is made more difficult in countries like the Islamic Republic of Iran, where Amnesty International is not able to conduct on-the-spot research or observe political trials, and where there is no domestic human rights body or independent Bar Association seeking to protect the rights of Iranian citizens.

In compiling data for this memorandum Amnesty International has used a wide range of sources, both official and unofficial. The organization has monitored the official Iranian news media, including the Official Gazette, as well as documentation produced by opposition groups of various political tendencies. It has interviewed scores of former prisoners, as well as relatives of prisoners, and has received written testimony from many others. Other people interviewed by Amnesty International include academics, jurists and journalists.

There are instances in this memorandum where Amnesty International quotes from personal testimonies it has collected. Some of these were given by members of and sympathizers with political groups opposing the Government of the Islamic Republic of Iran. Others were given by individuals who have never been members of any political group. All such testimony is included only where it demonstrates, in Amnesty International's view, a consistent pattern of treatment, and is typical of many other testimonies the organization has received. As requested, Amnesty International has not identified any of the individuals quoted. Many said they feared that if they were identified this could result in reprisals against members of their families still in Iran.

Where Amnesty International is unable to substantiate allegations of human rights abuses, it is careful to indicate this, and it frequently seeks clarification of reports of human rights violations from the appropriate authorities before making the information public. Amnesty International regrets that in most cases in which such clarification has been sought from the Government of the Islamic Republic of Iran no substantive response has been forthcoming.

Amnesty International's efforts to combat those human rights violations which fall within its terms of reference, as described above, relate specifically to violations committed or condoned by governments, which are bound by international human rights instruments as well as, in many instances, by domestic legislation to promote and protect the rights of their citizens. The organization does not condone any acts of violence or sabotage, whatever their nature, but believes that such acts should never be considered justification for any form of treatment or punishment which does not conform to international human rights standards.

Iran is a party to many international human rights instruments, among them the International Covenant on Civil and Political Rights, the International Covenant on Economic, Social and Cultural Rights, the Convention on the Prevention and Punishment of the Crime of Genocide and the Geneva Conventions of 12 August 1949, and Relating to the Protection of Victims of International Armed Conflicts. While these covenants and treaties were signed or ratified before the Islamic Republic came into being, their provisions are nevertheless binding on the present government. The Islamic Republic of Iran has clearly demonstrated that it considers itself bound by these commitments by appearing in 1982 before the Human Rights Committee examining its compliance with the provisions of the International Covenant on Civil and Political Rights. Furthermore, in December 1984 Iran's representative at the United Nations introduced a draft resolution to the Third Committee of the General Assembly which would have reaffirmed the importance of the United Nations Declaration against Torture. It would have recognized that new torture techniques and machinery "are detrimental to the fate of the individual and of the society as a whole", and it would have condemned all acts of torture and called for the prohibition of all means of torture, as well as their development, production and storage. Although this draft resolution was later withdrawn, it was a clear and positive indication that the Islamic Republic of Iran does not challenge the international legal obligation to prevent and prohibit the use of torture. Amnesty International believes that the Islamic Republic of Iran remains bound to honour and implement all the international legal instruments mentioned above.

Amnesty International regrets that since April 1979 it has been unable to send any mission to the Islamic Republic of Iran, although it has sought to send observers to attend political trials and delegates to hold talks with government and other authorities. On 22 October 1981 Amnesty International received a response from the Iranian Ministry of Foreign Affairs laying down certain conditions, including some of a political nature, to be met by the organization before a delegation would be received. Amnesty International was unable to accept the conditions proposed, and explained, in a letter to the Prime Minister, the policy and guidelines regulating its missions. It reiterated its wish, at that time, to discuss human rights violations with members of the government, and several times since has repeated its request to send a delegation to Tehran for high level talks.

Amnesty International regrets that no independent, impartial body working in the field of human rights has been allowed into the Islamic Republic of Iran for some time and notes that the Special Representative appointed by the United Nations to investigate human rights violations there was also denied entry. Amnesty International believes that the continued refusal by the Iranian Government to allow entry by international organizations concerned about human rights cannot dispel concern about the violation of these rights, and indeed only serves to aggravate it. Amnesty International trusts that the Government of the Islamic Republic of Iran will reconsider its position in this regard and demonstrate its willingness to cooperate with independent humanitarian and human rights bodies with a view to promoting and protecting the human rights of all Iranian citizens.

This memorandum, while noting Amnesty International's concerns with regard to the Islamic Republic of Iran, also includes a series of recommendations which Amnesty International believes could, if carried out, constitute concrete steps towards achieving greater protection against infringement of human rights. In submitting this document to the Islamic Republic of Iran, Amnesty International once again respectfully renews its proposal to hold talks in Tehran, and states that it would welcome the opportunity to discuss, in particular, the contents of this memorandum.

2. Political arrest and imprisonment

Amnesty International believes that there are at present many thousands of political prisoners in the Islamic Republic of Iran, but cannot estimate how many of them are possible prisoners of conscience. They include writers, journalists, doctors, lawyers, lecturers and teachers, students, housewives, factory and manual workers. Some are very old (sometimes aged over 70), some are in their teens and were still at school at the time of their arrest.

Victims of arrest since the February 1979 revolution cover the entire political spectrum, ranging from communists to members of monarchist groups. Among those at present in prison in the Islamic Republic of Iran are members and supporters of the Democratic

Party of Kurdistan of Iran, *Komeleh*, the People's *Feda'i* Organization of Iran, the People's *Mojahedine* Organization of Iran (PMOI), *Rah-e Kargar*, the *Tudeh* Party, and the Union of Communists, as well as members and supporters of groups who support the return to power of the monarchy. Also imprisoned are members of the Baha'i faith.

Amnesty International acknowledges that some political prisoners, including prisoners of conscience, have benefited from amnesties or reductions in sentences of imprisonment. However, it opposes unreservedly the incarceration of any individual for the non-violent expression of his or her conscientiously held beliefs, and calls for the immediate and unconditional release of the many people thus imprisoned in the Islamic Republic of Iran.

2.1 Law enforcement agencies with responsibility for effecting political arrests

In the overwhelming majority of cases of political arrest brought to the organization's attention in recent years, the arrests have been effected by the Islamic Revolutionary Guards Corps (IRGC) and Islamic Revolutionary Committee (*Komiteh*) (IRC) members. However, Amnesty International has also been informed that political arrests have been made by military and other personnel.

According to Article 150 of Iran's Constitution:

"The Corps of Guards of the Islamic Revolution,
established in the early days of the triumph of the
Revolution, is to be maintained in order that it may continue
in its role of guarding the Revolution and its achievements.
The duties of this Corps, together with its areas of responsibility, in relation to the duties and areas of responsibility of
the other armed forces, are to be determined by law, with
emphasis on brotherly cooperation and harmony among
them."

Ettela'at (25 August1985) quoted Hojatoleslam Salek, deputy chief of the Islamic Revolutionary Committee, defining their area of competence as follows:

"IRCs would be responsible for protecting public places,
and sensitive facilities, dealing with crimes relating to
intelligence, security and anti-revolutionaries, anti-narcotics
drive, anti-corruption drive, riots control, unauthorized
demonstrations, and anti-revolutionary disorders..."

Over the years, the IRGC's growth appears to have been matched by the increasing scope of its competence, until it became a powerful and virtually autonomous body, largely unaccountable to any higher authority for its actions.

One woman, whose testimony is typical of many in Amnesty International's possession, told Amnesty International what happened when Revolutionary Guards came to her Tehran home in November 1983 in search of her husband, a suspected political opposition activist:

> "Four armed guards came to my front door asking if this was my husband's home. When I said it was, they rushed inside. [They all carried IRGC identity cards.] I was there with my three children, aged 11, eight and six months, my sister-in-law and her two children. They put us all in one room and locked the door. Then they searched the place. Finally they let me out to question me. They asked me about my husband, his education, age and profession. I explained he was away on business. They took photographs of him and phoned their headquarters with his description. The children were crying all the time. My young son had had a tooth out that morning and his mouth was still bleeding, but they wouldn't let me take him to the doctor. Each time there was a knock at the front door, and this was quite often as I have good neighbours, each guard would crouch in a corner of the room with their guns pointing towards the door as they sent me to answer it. The guards were changed at intervals of about two hours. When my brother arrived they took him to another room for questioning, and later took him away. The following day at 1pm they brought him back. When the guards had searched the place they took away computers, books, pens, anything they took a fancy to — they even took away children's books. When they brought my brother back it was to take me in his place. My children were crying and holding on to me but the guards pushed them aside and told me I was to take my young baby with me. When we reached Evin Prison they blindfolded me and took my child away. Then they took me to an interrogation hall and I had to go up some steps. I could feel that there were people coming down and I lifted my head to try to see under the blindfold, but they hit me hard on the head when I did this. Still I managed to see someone sitting in a wheel-chair, who looked almost comatose, with his legs bound together. Once we'd gone upstairs, we then went down to a basement and I could hear that my child was being carried nearby. She was crying."

Article 31 of the Administrative Regulations Governing the

Revolutionary Courts and Public Prosecutors Offices (published in Official Gazette No. 10039-2-/5/1358 dated 30/4/58) lays down basic guidelines on the limitations of the IRGC:

> "Revolutionary Guards are not authorized to arrest anyone without the written permission of the Public Prosecutor. Likewise they are not allowed to enter anyone's house or seize anyone's property without the written permission of the Public Prosecutor. In case of a violation of this article they shall be dismissed upon the order of the Revolutionary Public Prosecutor. If their act is regarded as a crime they shall be prosecuted by the Revolutionary Public Prosecutor's office."

Amnesty International has accumulated numerous reports describing arbitrary arrest and detention by IRGC members, not only without any form of written authorization but also often involving acts of brutality towards the person being detained and his or her relatives, accompanied by insults and threats, and frequently followed by systematic physical and/or psychological torture.

The treatment described in the following testimony was by no means unusual:

> "One night at about 2.30am [September 1981], a young man came to the door. He was dressed in civilian clothes. He asked to speak to my son. I told him to come back in the morning, but he insisted. Suddenly he took out a pocket radio and I heard someone say: 'You'd better go in.' Guards appeared on all three sides. Some were even on the roof. There were 11 armed guards inside the house and more outside. I couldn't see how many. They beat me up because I hadn't wanted to let them in, and burst into my wife's bedroom. She told them that if they were good Muslims they should wait till she was dressed, but they hurled vulgar insults at her, and then called me a homosexual. They threw my wife out of bed and dragged my son in by the hair and beat him. Afterwards they took him straight to Evin Prison. The rest of the family was taken to the IRGC office in west Tehran. My wife and young daughter were released the next day. They kept me in for a week, beating me every day and deprived me of food for the first three days. My son is still in Evin."

In such cases it is impossible to tell whether the conduct of the IRGC had been authorized by the Public Prosecutor. What is clear, however, is that disregard of proper procedures has occurred and this has been officially recognized. In December 1982 the then

Revolutionary Prosecutor General, Moussavi Tabrizi, issued a circular addressed to all revolutionary prosecutors throughout Iran:

"You must absolutely refrain from giving general warrants to Revolutionary Guards or *Komitehs* for the search of houses or shops, or for the arrest, summoning or imprisonment of persons. If such an order has been issued so far, declare it as null and void..." (*Keyhan*, 18 December 1982)

Despite this directive, however, a former Islamic Revolutionary judge told Amnesty International:

"The IRGC is an absolute power in Iran. Theoretically, on security and intelligence matters, they receive orders from the Prosecutor's office, but in fact the IRGC can even bring about the transfer or removal of the *hakem-e-shar'* [religious judge] or the Friday Imam [prayer leader]. They have created an atmosphere whereby even the *hukkam-e shar'* are cautious in their dealings with them. They consult the IRGC when issuing a verdict and even when passing sentence..."

Amnesty International welcomes the public recognition by some Iranian officials, including Ayatollah Montazeri, of the excesses committed by the IRGC and *Komiteh* members, including the following example which was reported by the Tehran Home Service on 30 January 1984 (translated and published in the BBC Summary of World Broadcasts, 1 February 1984 — MZ/7555/A/1):

"[The] accused being arrested by the guards should not be arrested by the guards on their own initiative but only under orders from a court. The revolution guards corps has no authority to insult the accused persons, their families or their dependants. The accused should be handed over to the court with due respect and, in cases where an order has been issued regarding the accused by a court, only that order should be carried out and nothing more...

"I have repeatedly said that the revolution guards and all other officials should not just on mere suspicion of a plot against the revolution engage in any anti-*Shari'a* acts by entering private homes or by arresting private individuals just out of curiosity. The *Qur'an* says: 'Do not be suspicious or curious...'

"It is acknowledged that some people might be engaged in anti-*Shari'a* activities in their homes but Islam does not allow officials to swarm over that home and drag the owner somewhere for questioning. We may only detain people engaged in illegal demonstrations in the streets."

Amnesty International respectfully recommends an urgent and thorough review of training procedures prescribed for all law enforcement officials in the Islamic Republic of Iran. Such training should take into account the directives laid down in the United Nations Code of Conduct for Law Enforcement Officials (adopted by the United Nations General Assembly on 17 December 1979), and it should be made clear that any member of any agency found responsible for committing such abuses of authority as are described above, is to be brought to justice and duly disciplined. In this respect Amnesty International would draw particular attention to Article 2 of the Code which states:

"In the performance of their duty, law enforcement officials shall respect and protect human dignity and maintain and uphold the human rights of all persons."

and Article 3 which states:

"Law enforcement officials may use force only when strictly necessary and to the extent required for the performance of their duty."

2.2 Arbitrary arrest

"No one can be arrested except in accordance with judgment and the procedure established by law. In the case of arrest, charges and supporting evidence must be communicated immediately in writing to the prisoner and be elucidated to him... Punishments for the infringement of these principles will be determined by law." (Article 32 of the Constitution of the Islamic Republic of Iran of 15 November 1979.)

In examining the application of arrest and detention procedures, particularly as regards political suspects in the Islamic Republic of Iran, Amnesty International has interviewed a considerable number of former prisoners of widely differing political views and backgrounds arrested in various parts of the country. It is Amnesty International's view, based on these testimonies and information gathered from other appropriate sources, that arrests in political/security cases are frequently arbitrary, and made regardless of the provisions of Article 32 of the Constitution.

Article 9 (1) of the International Covenant on Civil and Political Rights, ratified by Iran in 1975, stipulates that: "Everyone has the right to liberty and security of person. No one shall be subjected to arbitrary arrest or detention..."; Article 9 (2) states: "Anyone who is arrested shall be informed, at the time of arrest, of the reasons for his arrest and shall be promptly informed of any charges against him."

In practice political detainees often remain ignorant of the reason for their arrest for days, weeks or months. Many arrests are believed to have been made because detained friends, relatives or political colleagues had given the individual's name under torture. Amnesty International also knows of people arrested by mistake because their names were similar to those of political activists sought by the police, and of relatives and occasionally whole families being held hostage when a relative who was being sought could not be found. A former prisoner told Amnesty International about one man brought to the prison where he was held in Gorgan who was aged about 60, was having cardiac treatment in hospital, and was carried in on a stretcher. He remained in the prison for two days before the prison authorities realized that although his name was similar to that of a known political activist, he was not that person. He was then returned to the hospital.

Often an individual is arrested at home, being informed that he or she has to answer some questions, which may require absence for some hours, a period which in practice may extend to many months or even years in detention. Arrest may be accompanied by insults and threats not only to the victim but also to the victim's relatives, who are frequently advised by the arresting authorities not to make inquiries about the circumstances of the arrested person, and threatened with imprisonment themselves if they choose to disregard this advice.

When an arrest is made away from the victim's home the victim usually has no chance to inform relatives about the situation or his or her whereabouts and, when approached, the arresting authorities may deny that the individual is in their custody. It is not uncommon for families to search for the whereabouts of a "missing" relative for some months without receiving any official notification of the latter's arrest and detention. Relatives go in person to each prison, IRGC centre and *Komiteh* in the district, attempting to establish the missing person's whereabouts before, in some cases, receiving a telephone call confirming that he or she is in detention. This process may take several months. In Amnesty International's opinion the prevention of communication between a detained person and his or her relatives significantly increases the chances of the detainee being tortured or ill-treated, and also causes prolonged, unnecessary anguish for both the detainee and his or her family. Such practice is contrary to Rule 92 of the United Nations Standard Minimum Rules for the Treatment of Prisoners, which states:

"An untried prisoner shall be allowed to inform immediately his family of his detention and shall be given all reasonable facilities for communicating with his family and friends, and for receiving visits from them, subject only to such restrictions and supervision as are necessary in the interests of the administration of justice and of the security and good order of the institution."

In examining the practice of arbitrary arrest in the Islamic Republic of Iran, Amnesty International notes with concern the single article approved by the Supreme Judicial Council on 3 May 1983 which provides for the imprisonment or exile from two months to two years of anyone "having a record of committing crimes, whether or not they again commit crimes". While the crimes indicated appear to involve the use of violence and other behaviour which would not normally fall within Amnesty International's terms of reference, Amnesty International considers there are insufficient procedural and other safeguards to rule out the possibility of individuals being detained because of their political or other conscientiously held beliefs. Amnesty International considers such legislation a violation of Article 9 (1) of the International Covenant on Civil and Political Rights which forbids arbitrary arrest and detention, and that as such it should be repealed.

Amnesty International has documented cases of relatives apparently being seized and held hostage when the political suspect concerned could not be found. In most such cases it has been the wives of suspected political activists who have escaped arrest who have been affected. One victim of such treatment told Amnesty International:

"The Revolutionary Guards came to our home in Esfahan in November 1983. They were looking for my husband but had no warrant with them, and my husband had already managed to leave the country. When they couldn't find my husband they said they just wanted to take me for a couple of hours to ask me a few questions. My father and younger sister, aged 19, were taken along too but they were released after six hours. I remained in prison for 14 months..."

Amnesty International believes this practice is still prevalent in the Islamic Republic of Iran. The organization learned of a case in 1985 in which a woman was arrested in Tehran and sentenced to seven years' imprisonment when her husband could not be traced. It was apparently made clear to her that if her husband were to be found in Iran she would be released. She is believed at present to be in Qezel-Hesar Prison.

Amnesty International knows of cases in which entire families have been rounded up:

"I was arrested in September 1980. The Revolutionary
Guards came to our home and searched it. My father,
mother, sister and younger brother were there and they
locked them in a room together. When I got home my
brother had also just returned and neither of us knew what
was going on. Our house had a cellar and they took the two
of us there and beat us up. There were 10 or 12 of them.
Then they took the whole family to the Revolutionary
Guards headquarters in Orumiyeh. Fortunately we managed
to persuade them to release our parents after a few days..."

Such practice is contrary to Article 9 (1) of the International
Covenant on Civil and Political Rights, which Iran has ratified and
which forbids arbitrary arrest and detention. Amnesty International
would also respectfully point out that it is a principle common to all
legal systems that persons should not be punished for offences they
have not committed. Amnesty International therefore respectfully
recommends that, as a matter of urgency, such practice be
discontinued.

2.3   Detention

Amnesty International is concerned because even the most basic
safeguards for the treatment of prisoners in the Islamic Republic of
Iran are frequently lacking. There is no limit to the length of time for
which a person may be in incommunicado detention, and in
Amnesty International's experience torture or ill-treatment is,
regardless of other provisions or safeguards, more likely to occur
when the detainee is out of touch with the outside world for long
periods. There is even more cause for concern when the person
concerned is not acknowledged to be in detention and when the place
of detention itself is not publicly recognized as such. Amnesty
International knows that there are many places of detention in the
Islamic Republic of Iran which are not publicly recognized prisons.
In addition to buildings and offices formerly used by SAVAK (secret
police) during the Shah's time, Amnesty International knows of
schools, houses, offices and even a theatre which have been
transformed into places of detention.

Article 9 (3) of the International Covenant on Civil and Political
Rights states that:

"Anyone arrested or detained on a criminal charge shall be
brought promptly before a judge or other officer authorized
by law to exercise judicial power and shall be entitled to trial
within a reasonable time or to release..."

Amnesty International believes that this right is completely disregarded in practice.

Because of the lack of a legal time-limit for incommunicado detention, individuals may be kept thus without trial for many weeks or months. Some former detainees have told Amnesty International that the authorities detaining them hoped that they would confess their "crimes" under physical or psychological torture, or give information about political colleagues, or that some detainees would divulge information about their political beliefs or activities. Thus in the course of someone's detention sufficient information would emerge on which to base charges and a subsequent conviction. Occasionally, after spending months in detention a detainee is informed of his or her release without charge or trial, but often on condition that he or she sign an undertaking not to become involved in any political activities, relatives sometimes pledging money or property as guarantees.

At no time during the arrest and detention procedures, or during trial, do detainees have access to legal counsel. They are thus entirely cut off from family, friends and legal advice; and as a rule they are also denied major medical attention or treatment, not allowed reading materials or to listen to the radio and prevented from writing or receiving correspondence. They may also spend their initial period of detention in solitary confinement. Again in practice there appears to be no limit to such periods of isolation.

Detainees may be interrogated immediately on arrival, or simply left alone in a cell with a pen and a sheet of paper and instructed to write about their "problems" or their life histories, plus the names of all the political activists they know. This may then form the basis for interrogation. If so a detainee will probably be required, at the discretion of the detaining authority, to write and rewrite his or her confessions or life history. Some former detainees, however, have told Amnesty International that they were kept in a cell for several months before undergoing any form of questioning and that consequently they suffered from suspense and uncertainty.

The above situation, in Amnesty International's opinion, constitutes treatment which is unacceptable in the light of international standards on the treatment of untried prisoners.

The majority of detainees, moreover, have undergone other forms of physical and/or psychological torture or ill-treatment during detention. Furthermore, the period spent in detention is not taken into account when a prison sentence is served, hence the sentence begins on the day it is imposed, even if the detainee has already spent many months or years in pre-trial detention, and Amnesty International has also recorded cases where individuals remain in prison, even though their prison term has been completed.

3. Torture and other cruel, inhuman or degrading treatment or punishment

Torture in the Islamic Republic of Iran remains of major concern to Amnesty International. The organization has received hundreds of reports of torture and ill-treatment in Iranian prisons and detention centres in recent years. The detailed nature of these reports, their number and their consistency have forced Amnesty International to conclude that torture, both physical and psychological, has been commonly inflicted, and at certain periods in certain prisons and detention centres has been a routine practice.

Amnesty International has interviewed in depth scores of torture victims who have fled the country and become refugees in various European and other countries. Some were members or supporters of various political groups, although a number had not been engaged in any political activity but had been arrested only on suspicion or because they had voiced some sort of criticism or else simply by mistake. Others arrested and tortured were members of the Baha'i faith.

Some of these individuals were medically examined by doctors at the request of Amnesty International. In every case, the doctor concluded from the examination that the nature of the physical scarring sustained and the symptoms described by the examinee were consistent with the methods of torture alleged and with the time at which torture was claimed to have occurred. Physical scarring was almost always accompanied by psychological disorders, and torture victims examined consistently complained of such symptoms as inability to concentrate, insomnia and feelings of insecurity and mistrust of others. Many suffered from emotional difficulties with regard to their family and other relationships. Such problems were often evident years after the torture had taken place.

Many methods of physical torture and ill-treatment have been described to Amnesty International by former prisoners. They include "football", a term which describes treatment used to intimidate and disorientate a detainee, often shortly after arrest. The blindfolded detainee, with wrists bound, is pushed violently from one guard to another, at the same time being punched, kicked, and beaten indiscriminately all over the body. Such treatment may then be followed by an initial interrogation.

Beating and suspension are the forms of torture most often reported, although the method of torture and the way in which it is inflicted may well vary according to the susceptibilities of the detainee concerned.

Beating is most frequently on the back, from the nape of the neck to the back of the thighs, and on the soles of the feet. All kinds of rope and cable have been used, including telephone wire, lengths of hosepipe, electricity cables with the naked wires teased into a ball at one end, plaited leather whips and a kind of steel cable opened out into a claw at one end. A recurring image in the many testimonies gathered by Amnesty International is that of rows of detainees sitting blindfold on the floor at Evin prison, with swollen, bleeding feet.

A young woman who was arrested in November 1983 when she was only 16 and was held until April 1985 told Amnesty International that when she was taken for interrogation in Evin prison:

"They blindfolded me and wrapped a blanket round my head, so I could see absolutely nothing. The lashes tore into the flesh on the soles of my feet, and I lost consciousness several times. Sometimes they poured water over them."

A man who was arrested at his home in Tehran in August 1982 told Amnesty International:

"They [Revolutionary Guards] put me in handcuffs which got tighter as I moved my hands. They were fastened behind my back, diagonally, one arm stretched over the shoulder and the other under. It is quite a mild form of torture but the effects are long-lasting and the pressure builds up gradually. In the end it's as though they're going to pull your shoulders off, and you feel your ribs will crack..."

Later he added:

"They suspended me [by the handcuffs] from a hook on the wall with only the tips of my toes touching the ground. At first, of course, I took some of the weight on my toes to ease the pain on my shoulders. But my feet had just been beaten and they were also swollen and very painful. Gradually, as my legs became tired, my body slumped down and the pressure on my shoulders began. This happens after only a few minutes..."

Amnesty International has also received reports of various kinds of sexual abuse of both male and female prisoners, including rape.

Amnesty International has noted the well-publicized reports that young women prisoners have been forced into temporary marriage contracts with members of the IRGC and have subsequently been raped the night before their execution, and has been told of cases in which IRGC members approached the families of young women who had been executed to present the bride money. Amnesty International has noted also reports that IRGC members have boasted about such acts to male prisoners, or threatened to enter into temporary marriage contracts with their female relatives. While Amnesty International has not been able to substantiate such reports it seems clear that, irrespective of whether this practice does exist or has existed in the Islamic Republic of Iran, many former prisoners who have testified to Amnesty International believed these reports were true and themselves suffered the anguish, while in prison, of fearing that they or their female relatives were liable to receive such treatment.

Amnesty International has received numerous reports of burns, usually caused by a lighted cigarette applied to the body, as a form of torture. In one such case a man arrested on two occasions told Amnesty International that because of his political sympathies he was burned with cigarettes during both periods of imprisonment. Now in Europe, he was medically examined in 1985 for Amnesty International by doctors who concluded that: "The circular (3 to 5mm) areas within the scar support the allegation of the use of cigarettes."

Amnesty International has received a number of reports of deaths as a result of torture. In such cases the body is rarely returned to the family for burial, although Amnesty International has heard of one or two cases in which the prisoner was released with physical injuries after having been severely tortured and died some days later as a consequence.

Frequently torture victims have been denied adequate medical treatment. According to Amnesty International's information prisoners are not given a medical examination on arrival at the prison and often cannot receive even basic medical care. In some prisons aspirin or sedatives have been administered, or soothing ointment given to prisoners who have sustained injuries as a result of beatings or other forms of torture or ill-treatment; but many former prisoners have told Amnesty International that even these medicaments were lacking during their imprisonment. Some reports received by Amnesty International suggest that, in the absence of a qualified doctor working in the prison, treatment has been given by medical students, doctors who were themselves prisoners or guards trained to give rudimentary medical aid. Access to specialized medical treatment including hospital treatment has, in some cases, been denied or delayed for long periods.

Poor hygiene and insufficient sanitary facilities in prisons, compounded at times by severe overcrowding, have encouraged the spread of skin diseases, scabies and lice. Many former prisoners have complained of untreated kidney disorders due to beatings, and of other wounds — sustained through torture — becoming septic and malodorous through lack of medical attention and poor hygiene.

Psychological suffering too has been consistently and repeatedly described by former prisoners. Detainees have been kept in prolonged isolation, often experiencing a sense of loss of reality. They have experienced feelings of insecurity and vulnerability aggravated by blindfolding for long periods, and of anxiety and fear exacerbated by hearing the screams of other prisoners being tortured and by being kept ignorant of their fate. Feelings of humiliation and self-disgust are common.

A woman prisoner held in Evin prison and Gohar Dasht prison stated:

"Out of the 14 months I spent in prison I was in solitary confinement for nine months, either in solitary confinement in the strictest sense, or in cells intended for one person but where there were two or three of us. But for the nine months there was no contact whatsoever with the outside world, no reading material, nothing. In that period I tried to look after myself and take hold of myself because I could feel myself under pressure and becoming psychologically unbalanced at times... No one had questioned or interrogated me, I was still waiting for someone to question me, and this brought with it a lot of anxiety too. All the time I saw strange things, like pictures in my mind, and I felt that everybody was an informer. I imagined I saw my husband and that he was an interrogator and even, can you imagine, I thought my tiny son was one, too..."

Former prisoners have complained of pressure to repent of their actions or political affiliations, either through frequent religious speeches broadcast through loudspeakers, or by means of closed-circuit televised coverage of religious ceremonies within the prison confines, including interviews with repentant prisoners. Prisoners may be told that they will be released or that their conditions will improve only if they become truly repentant. Many have also been required to identify other members of their political group either within the prison or while being driven around the town, or to obtain information from fellow-prisoners, or to make a televised confession.

Some former prisoners have told Amnesty International how they were relieved to be approached in their cell by a fellow-prisoner, seemingly sympathetic and comforting, only to find that the latter was a repentant prisoner attempting to gather information on their political activities and contacts.

Detainees have been threatened with the rape or imprisonment of relatives, or with execution unless they supply information. Amnesty International has collected many accounts of mock executions, when the victims were ordered to write their wills and were blindfolded and prepared for execution. Guards fired shots all around them, then they were returned to their cells. One former detainee described the return, following mock execution, of a cell-mate who "looked like a dead man" because of the severe shock.

A former prisoner described his experience in 1982:

"They took me to a yard where there were four wooden posts in a semi-circle, and they tied each of us to a post. The first was a boy of 14 or 15, a member of the People's *Mojahedine* Organization of Iran (PMOI). The second was an army officer and the third, aged about 23, was a member of *Peykar*. I was the fourth. The time before, when they asked if I had a last wish, I asked them to remove my blindfold, so this time they didn't blindfold me. I saw the bullet hit the PMOI boy and the officer was hit in the stomach. The *Peykar* man may already have been dead, his body didn't react to the bullet. The young boy was shaking violently with a bullet in his body. His hands were tied and he was trying with all his might to free himself. He was bleeding profusely. I shouted 'What are you waiting for? Why don't you shoot me?' They laughed, and I could do nothing. The young boy died, then the officer. I had just stood there and watched them suffering... I try very hard not to remember."

Other prisoners have testified to the psychological effects of loading the bodies of executed prisoners onto lorries. Amnesty International knows of cases in which prisoners have been forced to witness the execution of political colleagues, or have been shown the tortured body of a relative or spouse.

A member of the Baha'i faith, imprisoned in Shiraz in early 1983, told Amnesty International about a young woman prisoner there at the same time who was informed by prison guards that her husband had been severely tortured but that this would end if she agreed to recant her faith. When she refused she was taken to see him and was shocked at his condition. He had lost weight drastically, had bleeding, running sores on his back and his toe nails had been removed. Husband and wife, both Baha'is, were later executed.

In such circumstances many prisoners have suffered serious psychological and emotional disorders and some have reported that disturbed prisoners were deliberately put with them in their cells to increase their own distress.

Amnesty International recognizes that the ordering and infliction of physical ill-treatment is a punishable offence under Iranian law, and that the Constitution of the Islamic Republic of Iran forbids the use of "any form of torture for the purpose of extracting confessions or gaining information..." (Article 38). However, during the past five years Amnesty International has collected so many and such consistent reports of severe torture that it believes immediate further measures are needed to prevent such treatment continuing. The organization recommends that such measures include:

(a) clear and publicized condemnation of the use of torture to be made by the highest authorities in the land;
(b) the holding of all detainees in publicly recognized places of detention or prisons, not in secret places;
(c) the strengthening and enforcement of legislation prohibiting torture;
(d) the bringing to justice of those responsible for inflicting or ordering torture and seeing this is known;
(e) the inclusion in the training programs of all law enforcement agencies of a strict and unequivocal prohibition of torture;
(f) the compensation of torture victims.

In view of both the gravity and the quantity of the allegations of torture and ill-treatment, both physical and psychological, received by Amnesty International, it recommends the establishment of an independent, impartial commission of inquiry into such allegations. Amnesty International is aware that an inquiry into torture was previously initiated in 1980 to 1981, but, in the light of reports received, considers a fresh inquiry already long overdue. It is therefore urging that every effort be made to ensure the protection of any victim or his or her family presenting evidence, because of intimidation or fear of reprisals. The commission of inquiry's terms of reference should include conducting a thorough review of all administrative and judicial procedures regulating the arrest, incarceration and interrogation of political suspects. The organization recommends also that the commission's findings and recommendations, as well as the procedures followed, be made public.

Pending the establishment of such a commission, Amnesty International urges that basic practical safeguards be immediately established, including a requirement to give clear information to the next of kin about the victim's arrest and whereabouts; to grant access for every detainee to relatives and a lawyer of his or her own choosing promptly after arrest and at brief, regular intervals thereafter. Every detainee should be examined by a qualified doctor on arrival in prison and a medical report written; a copy of the report (paying full regard to the confidentiality of its contents) should be held by a central authority. Frequent and unannounced visits by qualified people should be made to all prisons and detention centres so that they can record and seek redress for prisoners' complaints as well as monitor standards of medical treatment, food and hygiene. Copies of such records should be kept and studied by a central authority.

On 10 December 1984 the United Nations General Assembly adopted the Convention against Torture and Other Cruel, Inhuman or Degrading Treatment or Punishment, through Resolution 39/46, which called upon "... all Governments to consider signing and ratifying the Convention as a matter of priority". The Convention obliges all States Parties to make torture a punishable offence and to prevent the use of torture in their jurisdictions. Amnesty International respectfully urges the Government of the Islamic Republic of Iran immediately to accede to the Convention against Torture, which has so far been acceded to or ratified by 10 states and signed by 47 others.[1]

4. Right to fair trial

The lack of right to a fair trial for political prisoners in the Islamic Republic of Iran remains of major concern to Amnesty International. The organization's concern is all the more grave because of the wide range of capital offences.

After the 1979 revolution a series of measures was adopted to transform the judicial system into one that would be consistent with *Shari'a*. All laws which did not conform with *Shari'a* were repealed, a new constitution was promulgated and preparations were made to draft a new penal code[2] and new penal procedure code.

Amnesty International realizes that the transition from secular to religious law is still going on, some seven years after the revolution. Among the major problems involved in this change was the shortage of qualified judges and the lack of a clear legal framework in which to operate. New legislation took time to draft and approve, and judges were frequently working in isolation, often without either experience or legal qualifications (or neither) and without a coherent

---

[1] As of 1 November 1986

[2] On 8 August 1986 Amnesty International sent a memorandum concerning the Islamic Penal Code of Iran to the Islamic Republic of Iran for consideration and comment.

body of laws defining offences and the scope of punishments. Such factors combined to create an almost entirely arbitrary system for the administration of justice with widely disparate sentences being passed in different parts of the country for the same offences, and with a system offering little or no possibility of redressing the many wrongs that inevitably resulted.

Basic Principle 10 of the United Nations Basic Principles on the Independence of the Judiciary requires:

"In the selection of judges, there shall be no discrimination against a person on the grounds of race, colour, sex, religion, political or other opinion, national or social origin, property, birth or status, except that a requirement, that a candidate for judicial office must be a national of the country concerned, shall not be considered discriminatory."

The Basic Principles on the Independence of the Judiciary were adopted by the Seventh United Nations Congress on the Prevention of Crime and the Treatment of Offenders in September 1985, and were endorsed by the United Nations General Assembly in Resolution 40/32 of 29 November 1985.

The methods of judicial appointment should include safeguards against judicial appointments for improper motives and should ensure the non-discriminatory selection of individuals of integrity with appropriate training and qualifications in law. Any discrimination on grounds of sex and religion should be examined closely in order to prevent unfair proceedings in political cases, particularly cases against women or non-Muslims.

In fact Amnesty International has received numerous reports from throughout the country of young judges who had clearly not had adequate legal training conducting political trials.

Amnesty International is aware that numerous circulars and official statements issued since 1979 have referred to the lack of qualified judges and have introduced a series of interim measures to facilitate the administration of justice until such time as there are enough fully qualified judges.

According to a statement reported in *Ettela'at* in December 1985, Ayatollah Ruhollah Khomeini noted:

"... the overwhelming majority of those dealing in jurisprudence are not yet qualified by *Shari'a* for judicial affairs and have only been appointed as a measure to meet the exigencies of the time being; they are not therefore entitled to determine the punishment by *Ta'azir* without permission of the fully qualified *faqih* [Islamic juris- prudent]. Accordingly it is necessary that a committee be set

up, composed of the President of the Supreme Court of the country, the head of the judicial committee and two of the Guardian Council jurisprudents, in order to decide the limits of punishment by *Ta'azirat* on which basis punishment shall be authorized and violation thereof shall not be allowed.
This is to be considered a temporary and exigent measure until, by God's will, the fully qualified judges are appointed...''

Amnesty International welcomes such measures which can only contribute to a more uniform application of the law and help curb some of the more excessive punishments, which are disproportionate to the nature of the offence, and urges their speedy application. Amnesty International would therefore respectfully draw the attention of the above-mentioned committee in particular to Recommendation E.1 urging the relevant authorities to replace those punishments provided for by *Ta'azirat* which constitute forms of torture or cruel, inhuman or degrading treatment or punishment with other penalties consistent with international human rights standards.

4.1 Criminal courts

Amnesty International realizes that Criminal Courts One and Two are competent to hear cases defined by the laws of *Hodoud, Qesas, Diyat* and *Ta'azirat* which do not fall within the jurisdiction of the Islamic Revolutionary Courts, as described in 4.2.

Article 198 of the Penal Procedure Code, as amended, defines the jurisdiction of Criminal Court One as follows:

''(a) crimes, the punishment for which is the death sentence, stoning to death (*rajm*), cross amputation (*salb*), and exile;

(b) crimes the punishment for which is amputation

(c) crimes the punishment for which is 10 years' imprisonment or more, according to provisions of the law;

(d) crimes the punishment for which is equivalent to 2,000,000 rials [about £17,000] and over, or equivalent to two-fifths of the convicted person's property or more...''

Criminal Court One is composed of one president or alternate member and one adviser (Article 195 of the Penal Procedure Code as amended). Criminal Court Two is composed of one president or alternate member and is competent to deal with:

''Crimes for which the punishments are other than those

mentioned in Article 198... likewise all minor crimes and violations such as failure to observe the rules and regulations of the municipality, the police, or of health and hygiene, traffic... vagrancy, beggary, use of foul language and the like shall be examined by Criminal Court Two." (Article 217)

Article 289 of the Penal Procedure Code provides that:

"Judgments of criminal courts must be substantiated and plausible and must be based on articles of law and principles on the basis of which the judgment is passed. Courts are required to find out provisions on each problem in the legislated laws; in cases where no such law exists they will be required to pass judgment on the case under consideration on the basis of valid sources of *fiqh* [Islamic jurisprudence] or well-known and valid religious decrees."

According to Article 285 of the Penal Procedure Code, as amended, the Supreme Court is required to "discuss all views" of the criminal courts resulting in the punishments described above which fall within the competence of Criminal Court One. This process of review as provided for major offences in Article 285 would appear to be quite inadequate in the light of international standards for fair trial. No actual judgment is passed in the lower court and, as indicated in Article 287 of the Penal Procedure Code, as amended, the criminal courts send their views on how the cases should be resolved to the Supreme Court for approval. There is no provision in law for any contribution by the accused during the lower court's investigation, or during the review of the lower court's opinion.

According to Article 14 (3)(d) of the International Covenant on Civil and Political Rights everyone is entitled "to be tried in his presence, and to defend himself in person or through legal assistance of his own choosing". Judging by the provisions of Articles 285, 287 and 289 of the Penal Procedure Code, as described above, it would appear that those on trial have no right to defend themselves during the review of their cases which results in the final judgment.

Furthermore, according to Article 287 of the Penal Procedure Code, convictions involving lesser punishments are final and binding judgments against which those convicted cannot appeal. These punishments include imprisonment for up to 10 years.[3]

---

[3] Article 284 of the Penal Procedure Code stipulates the only three instances in which such a judgment may be revoked and revised:

1. Where the judge becomes certain that the judgment passed by him is contrary to

28

Consequently Amnesty International was particularly disturbed by a report in *Keyhan* on 12 April 1983 that mobile anti-narcotic courts were being set up whose procedures appeared to fall far short of international human rights standards. The article quotes Ayatollah Moussavi Ardebili, Chief Justice of the Supreme Court, as saying that the court is intended to deal with drug abuse on the spot, and that as the crime is obvious *(flagrens crimen)* the criminal is to undergo physical punishment, that is, be whipped on the spot. Some of the criminals may be sent to courts of law (of the Ministry of Justice) to be whipped there, if the religious judge so decides. The report went on to say that Ayatollah Ardebili regarded most drug smugglers as *mofsed fil arz* (corrupt on earth), and that for them the punishment is death. Another punishment he suggested was amputating criminals' right hands and left legs and leaving them to die.

4.2 Islamic Revolutionary Courts

Amnesty International realizes that Islamic Revolutionary Courts were created in 1979 as a temporary measure, mainly in order to try the cases of the numerous people arrested in connection with the Shah's administration.

The jurisdiction, procedure and composition of the Islamic Revolutionary Courts are enshrined in the 34 articles comprising the Administrative Regulations Governing the Revolutionary Courts and Public Prosecutors Offices[4] and published in Official Gazette No. 10039, having been approved by the then Islamic Revolutionary Council in June 1979. The scope of their jurisdiction since then has been amended[5] to comprise:

"1. All crimes against internal and external security, *Moharebeh* [enmity to God] and corruption on earth.

2. Attempts on the life of political personalities.

3. All crimes related to narcotics and smuggling.

4. Murder, killing, imprisoning and torturing for the purpose of consolidating the Pahlavi regime and suppressing the struggle of the people of Iran whether as

---

the provisions of the law or *Shari'a*.

2. Where another judge becomes certain that the judge made a mistake of law or *Shari'a* so that if he is warned he will understand his mistake.

3. Where it is proved that the judge was not competent to examine and pass judgment on the case.

[4]The Revolutionary Public Prosecutor's Office was merged with the Public Prosecutor's Office in early 1984.

[5]Approved in May 1983, and published in Official Gazette No. 11139.

an associate or as an accomplice.

5. Plunder of Public Treasury.
6. Profiteering and hoarding of general provisions.''

Article 4 of the Administrative Regulations referred to above stipulates that the court shall be composed of three principal and two alternate members, the principal members to be: a religious judge, proposed by the Islamic Revolutionary Council and approved by the Imam; a judge from the Ministry of Justice, appointed by the afore-mentioned judge; an individual "trusted by the people having been acquainted with the exigencies of the Islamic Revolutionary Council or someone designated for this purpose by the Council''. No member of the court is to be aged under 30, and the court is to be presided over by the religious judge. (Note 2 to Article 4, and Article 5, respectively, of the Administrative Regulations.)

According to information collected by Amnesty International, in practice these courts may well consist of a one-person tribunal, namely a religious judge. Indeed Amnesty International knows of no cases in which the three-member tribunal, as provided for in Article 4 of the Administrative Regulations, has functioned in political cases. Amnesty International has received many complaints that the judges concerned were students, insufficiently trained for their responsibilities.

General Comment 13 (21) by the Human Rights Committee on Article 14 of the International Covenant on Civil and Political Rights notes the existence in many countries of military or special courts which try civilians, but indicates that such proceedings "should be very exceptional and take place under conditions which genuinely afford the full guarantees stipulated in Article 14''. Islamic Revolutionary Courts deal with a wide range of major offences and in various ways do not make provision for the full procedural guarantees prescribed by Article 14 of the Covenant.

Article 6 of the Administrative Regulations Governing the Revolutionary Courts requires bills of indictment to be served on the accused or his or her attorney not later than three days before the trial, and Article 8 allows the court a maximum of a week in which to decide on the case. A note to this article adds that the attorney must be permitted 15 hours in which to conduct the defence. Although these provisions do give accused people and their attorneys some protection of the right to fair trial, they certainly would not give the former "the full guarantees stipulated in Article 14'', as required by the Human Rights Committee's General Comment referred to above. In any event, in practice Amnesty International knows of no single case in which the accused has been allowed any access to an attorney, nor any case in which the accused has been permitted 15 hours in which to offer his or her own defence before an Islamic Revolutionary Court. Indeed, the overwhelming majority of former prisoners interviewed by Amnesty International have claimed that their trials lasted a mere matter of minutes in their entirety. Article 14 (3)(b) of the International Covenant on Civil and Political Rights stipulates that everyone facing a criminal charge shall be entitled to "have adequate time and facilities for the preparation of his defence..." Amnesty International is concerned that, even if adhered to, Articles 6 and 8 of the Administrative Regulations do not allow sufficient time for the preparation of a defence, especially considering the seriousness of the charges which may be brought before the Revolutionary Courts and the potential sentences, which include death and imprisonment.

Article 14 (1) of the International Covenant on Civil and Political Rights stipulates that a trial should be public, unless exceptional circumstances require it to be held *in camera*. These special circumstances are described in Article 14 (1). Under Note 1 to Article 9 of the Administrative Regulations, however, the decision as to whether or not a hearing should be public rests entirely with the president of the court, who is not required to give the reasons for his decision. This unbridled discretion is inconsistent with international standards. Furthermore, while Article 14 (3)(d) guarantees the right of the accused to "be tried in his presence", Articles 9 (Note 2) and 10 state that proceedings may take place and judgment be passed in the absence of the accused.

According to Article 14 (5) of the International Covenant on Civil and Political Rights:

"Everyone shall have the right to his conviction and
sentence being reviewed by a higher tribunal according to
law."

Article 11 of the Administrative Regulations, however, precludes any such review.

Basic Principle 5 of the United Nations Basic Principles on the Independence of the Judiciary requires a degree of conduct, to apply to all courts, stating:

"Everyone shall have the right to be tried by ordinary courts
or tribunals using established legal procedures. Tribunals
that do not use the duly established procedures of the legal
process shall not be created to displace the jurisdiction
belonging to the ordinary courts or judicial tribunals."

Amnesty International is deeply concerned about the conduct of trials before Islamic Revolutionary Courts. It considers that the

Administrative Regulations Governing Revolutionary Courts contain inadequate provisions for ensuring fair trial, and in its experience even those safeguards provided for by law are not adhered to. Amnesty International realizes that these courts were created as a temporary measure only, and recommends that consideration now be given to abolishing them in order to consolidate all judicial proceedings in one system, which should make provision for all necessary safeguards for fair trial. Amnesty International respectfully recommends that such steps be considered in the context of any review of existing legislation.

4.3 International standards for fair trial

Article 14 of the International Covenant on Civil and Political Rights, ratified by Iran, lays down basic provisions for fair trial in seven paragraphs. While certain of these provisions are reflected in Iranian legislation, Amnesty International believes that in practice not one of the seven can be considered totally adhered to as regards political cases tried by Islamic Revolutionary Courts in Iran.

1) Paragraph 1 of Article 14 begins "All persons shall be equal before the courts and tribunals..." This provision may be considered to have been breached in both law and practice in Iran, where there is religious and sexual discrimination.

Amnesty International has no information suggesting there is discriminatory treatment of women defendants in political trials, but the provisions of the Islamic Penal Code of Iran provide ample evidence to show that men and women are not treated equally by all courts in Iran. The section of the Penal Code on *Diyat* (compensation or blood-money for murder or injury) provides, among other things, that:

> "Blood-money for the murder of a Muslim woman, whether premeditated or unpremeditated, is half the blood-money of a Muslim male." (Article 6)

Elsewhere, in the *Hodoud* and *Qesas* section of the Islamic Penal Code of Iran, the testimony of women is shown to be of less value than that of men, for example, in cases of intentional murder only the testimony of two "righteous males" is admissible, while quasi-intentional murder is proved by the testimony of "two righteous males, or one righteous male and two righteous females..." (Article 33 (a) and (b), respectively.) The testimony of women on their own or together with a man is not admissible as proof of sodomy (Article 150).

Discrimination on religious grounds has been demonstrated

consistently in judicial proceedings as regards members of the Baha'i faith, many of whom have been executed for their refusal to recant their faith.

One example of discrimination on religious grounds was the judgment by Branch 146 of Criminal Court One of Tehran on 22 June 1985 that a Muslim driver who had killed a Baha'i in a traffic accident, while guilty of manslaughter, was under no obligation to the family of the victim, because he was a Baha'i.

According to another judgment, passed by Branch 13 of Criminal Court One of Shiraz on 23 December 1985, a Muslim who had delivered "a premeditated blow" to a Baha'i, resulting in his death, should not be prosecuted, neither could any retribution be claimed by the victim's family because of their faith.

Paragraph 1 of Article 14 also stipulates that "everyone shall be entitled to a fair and public hearing by a competent, independent and impartial tribunal established by law..." Almost no political trials are held in public, although occasionally there have been public sessions. However, Amnesty International knows of no such cases since the trial of those accused of belonging to the military branch of the Tudeh Party in January 1984. Such cases are exceptional, and Amnesty International believes that normally political trials are held *in camera*, no provision being made for the family of the accused or for defence counsel of any kind to attend.

The Human Rights Committee, in General Comment 13 (21) on this part of Article 14 of the Covenant stated:

"The publicity of hearings is an important safeguard in the interest of the individual and of society at large. At the same time Article 14, paragraph 1, acknowledges that courts have the power to exclude all or part of the public for reasons spelt out in that paragraph. It should be noted that, apart from such exceptional circumstances, the Committee considers that a hearing must be open to the public in general, including members of the press, and must not, for instance, be limited only to a particular category of persons..."

Basic Principle 2 on the Independence of the Judiciary defines independence as judges being free to:

"...decide matters before them impartially, on the basis of the facts and in accordance with the law, without any restriction, improper influence, inducements, pressure, threats or interferences, direct or indirect, from any quarter or for any reason."

Articles 57 and 156 of the Constitution of the Islamic Republic of

Iran are consistent with these international norms of judicial independence. According to Article 57, the sovereign powers on the Islamic Republic of Iran consist of the legislature, the executive and the judiciary, "which are independent of each other".

Legislation concerning courts in the Islamic Republic of Iran, however, contains provisions which would appear to influence or interfere with the independence of the judiciary. These provisions relate mainly to the qualifications required of judges, and procedures for appeal and review, particularly as regards Islamic Revolutionary Courts.

Paragraph 1 of Article 14 of the International Covenant on Civil and Political Rights goes on to say:

"... any judgment rendered in a criminal case or in a suit at law shall be made public except where the interest of juvenile persons otherwise requires, or the proceedings concern matrimonial disputes or the guardianship of children."

This matter is emphasized in the Human Rights Committee's General Comment 13 (21):

"... It should be noted that, even in cases in which the public is excluded from the trial, the judgment must, with certain strictly defined exceptions, be made public."

The above-described exceptions do not apply to cases which concern Amnesty International. However, in spite of these requirements, to which Iran is committed through its ratification of the Covenant, Amnesty International knows of many cases in which the judgment has not been made public, and indeed it would appear that in certain instances there have been clear directives to conceal the judgment. One case in point emerges in the following extract from a circular issued in 1982 by the Revolutionary Prosecutor General, addressed to all Revolutionary Prosecutors:

"... In cases where the crimes of individuals are proved and established before the courts of law and *Shari'a* courts, only the punishment imposed in the judgment should be carried out, and it must not be divulged or announced through the mass media, except in the case of the *mohareb* [at enmity with God] groups..." (*Keyhan*, 18 December 1982).

Amnesty International has recorded many cases in which the defendants were not informed of their conviction and sentence until days or weeks after the trial was over. Some were later told by their visiting relatives, others had heard "rumours" about their sentence. Few judgments in political cases appear to be officially and publicly announced.

2) Paragraph 2 of Article 14 of the Covenant states:

"Everyone charged with a criminal offence shall have the
right to be presumed innocent until proved guilty according
to law."

The apparently summary nature of trials by Islamic Revolutionary
Courts would strongly suggest that there is no presumption of the
defendants' innocence. Some former prisoners interviewed by
Amnesty International were even told by the Islamic judge that their
mere presence in the court was sufficient indication of their guilt.
Others were informed that their guilt had been proved by their
confessions, even though these had been extracted under torture.
This constitutes contravention, not only of the International
Covenant on Civil and Political Rights, but also of Iran's
Constitution, which provides, under Article 37, that:

"Innocence is to be presumed, and no one is to be regarded
as guilty unless his guilt has been established by the
competent court."

3) Paragraph 3 of Article 14 of the Covenant is sub-divided into
seven sub-paragraphs, which are considered to supply "minimum
guarantees" when deciding on charges. It provides that everyone
shall be entitled:

"(a) To be informed promptly and in detail in a language
which he understands of the nature and cause of the charge
against him."

Amnesty International does not believe this provision has been
applied with regard to political detainees in the Islamic Republic of
Iran. Indeed, the organization knows of individuals who were held
for months without any form of interrogation or indication of the
reason for their detention, much less of any formal charge against
them. Others have told Amnesty International that they were
accused of membership or holding office in several illegal political
movements simultaneously, in an attempt to force them to confess to
political activities in one of them. Many others believed that they had
been arrested because they had been known to be politically active
during the time of the late Shah and that since they were not visibly
active in support of the present government, they were assumed to
have resumed anti-government political activity.

This constitutes a breach of Article 32 of the Constitution, which
states:

"... charges and supporting evidence must be communicated
immediately in writing to the prisoner and be elucidated to
him..."

Sub-paragraph (b) of Article 14 (3) of the Covenant provides that everyone shall be entitled:

"To have adequate time and facilities for the preparation of his defence and to communicate with counsel of his own choosing."

In its General Comment 13 (21) on this sub-paragraph the Human Rights Committee has stated:

"... the facilities must include access to documents and other evidence which the accused requires to prepare his case, as well as the opportunity to engage and communicate with counsel... (T)his sub-paragraph requires counsel to communicate with the accused in conditions giving full respect for the confidentiality of their communications. Lawyers should be able to counsel and to represent their clients in accordance with their established professional standards and judgment without any restrictions, influences, pressures or undue interference from any quarter."

Amnesty International knows of no single case since 1979 in which anyone accused of a political offence has been permitted to contact or have access to defence counsel of his or her own choosing, or indeed to any legally qualified person acting in his or her interests. Amnesty International considers prompt and regular access to a defence lawyer of the accused's own choosing should be an essential part of the preparation of any trial. Moreover, prompt and regular access to a lawyer serves as basic protection for the detainee from being subjected to torture, cruel, inhuman or degrading treatment or punishment. This is particularly important during the period immediately following arrest and during subsequent interrogations.

"(c) To be tried without undue delay."

The Human Rights Committee's General Comment 13 (21) notes, with regard to sub-paragraph (c), that:

"To make this right effective a procedure must be available in order to ensure that the trial will proceed 'without undue delay', both in first instance and on appeal."

As already indicated in this document, there seems to be no legal limit in the Islamic Republic of Iran to pre-trial detention, and Amnesty International continues to receive reports of prolonged detention without charge or trial. Moreover, the amount of time spent in pre-trial detention is not taken into account for those serving a custodial sentence. An example of prolonged detention without trial is that of the woman prisoner, whose testimony appears on page 21, who was tried after she spent more than 13 months in prison without charge. Others are believed to have been held for more than three years without trial.

Amnesty International realizes that the Penal Procedure Code has yet to be promulgated *in toto* and strongly urges that safeguards be established to limit pre-trial detention and detention without trial, and to provide the right to challenge detention before a judicial authority.

> "(d) To be tried in his presence, and to defend himself in
> person or through legal assistance of his own choosing; to be
> informed, if he does not have legal assistance, of this right;
> and to have legal assistance assigned to him, in any case
> where the interests of justice so require, and without
> payment by him in any such case if he does not have
> sufficient means to pay for it."

As noted on page 30, Iranian law permits trials to be conducted by Islamic Revolutionary Courts in the absence of the accused and allows review by the Supreme Court, following trial by a criminal court, also to take place in the absence of the accused or his or her lawyer.

The Human Rights Committee stresses this provision in its General Comment 13 (21):

> "The accused or his lawyer must have the right to act
> diligently and fearlessly in pursuing all available defences
> and the right to challenge the conduct of the case if they
> believe it to be unfair..."

This right is among those guaranteed by Iran's own legislation. Article 35 of the Constitution states:

> "Both parties to a dispute have the right in all courts of law
> to select a lawyer, and if they are unable to do so, arrange-
> ments must be made to provide them with legal counsel."

Furthermore, according to Article 7 of the Administrative Regulations Governing the Revolutionary Courts and Public Prosecutor's Office:

> "Every accused person will have the right to appoint one
> Iranian attorney being acquainted with legal problems and
> Islamic penal laws."

These provisions and guarantees have been consistently breached as regards political detainees. Amnesty International knows of no cases since the February 1979 revolution in which lawyers have been able to defend a political detainee. In 1981 the Bar Association was forcibly ejected from its offices, and its documents seized. In early 1982 members of the elected Bar Council, including the President, were arrested, one of them remaining in prison in 1986. Other Bar Council members were forced into living clandestinely or in exile. Many practising lawyers were arrested and executed.

The organization is aware of a religious decree (reportedly passed in 1982 following questions addressed to Ayatollah Khomeini, Ayatollah Montazeri and Ayatollah Gholpayegani about the *Shari'a*) which states:

"According to the rules of holy Islam it shall be permissible to vest power of attorney in others, either for representation in courts or for other purposes."

The organization is aware also of the precedent established by the General Board of the Supreme Court under Precedent No. 71/62 Decision No. 15 in 1984:

"In the name of God the Almighty

"In view of the fact that Article 35 of the Constitution of the Islamic Republic of Iran has given special significance to the right of using attorney, and also in light of Article 9 of the Law on the Establishment of Criminal Courts, inference made from the regulations on Note 2, Article 7 and Article 12 on the Legal Bill on the Establishment of Public Courts ratified on 11 September 1979, and later amendments made in it under circular dated 9 October 1982 of the Guardians' Council are legally valid, involvement of the counsel briefed by the Government, 'in case the accused may not have personally named an attorney' is essential in cases where the main punishments of that crime could be death sentence or life imprisonment.

"... This precedent shall be binding on all benches of the Supreme Court and other courts in all similar cases in accordance with the Single Article of the Law on Judicial Precedent ratified in 1949."

Amnesty International welcomes this precedent and urges its immediate implementation by all courts in the Islamic Republic of Iran. It also recommends that the right to defence counsel be recognized as an inalienable right of any accused person before any court of law in the country.

"(e) To examine, or have examined, the witnesses against him and to obtain the attendance and examination of witnesses on his behalf under the same conditions as the witnesses against him."

The Human Rights Committee notes in General Comment 13 (21) that:

> "This provision is designed to guarantee to the accused the same legal powers of compelling the attendance of witnesses and of examining or cross-examining any witnesses as are available to the prosecution."

Amnesty International knows of political cases, particularly in the months following the revolution, in which witnesses were allowed to testify for the prosecution during trials, but knows of no such cases in which witnesses for the defence were permitted. Trials before Islamic Revolutionary Courts seem to dispense with witnesses entirely, despite the provision contained in Article 9 of the Administrative Regulations Governing Revolutionary Courts and Public Prosecutors Offices for "witnesses, informed persons and experts" to be summoned to court "if their presence is necessary" (there is no indication as to how to decide on the criteria for this necessity).

> "(f) To have the free assistance of an interpreter if he cannot understand or speak the language used in court."

Amnesty International has recorded some cases of individuals being tried in Iran on political grounds who reportedly could not communicate in Farsi and where no interpreter was available. One example reportedly involved a group of about 14 Iranian Arabs tried in late 1980, 13 of whom were sentenced to death and executed. None had understood the proceedings or been able to defend themselves, and no provision was made to provide interpreters for them.

With regard to the final sub-paragraph,

> "(g) Not to be compelled to testify against himself or to confess guilt."

Amnesty International has at its disposal a considerable body of evidence indicating that the accused has consistently been compelled to confess guilt as a result of physical and/or psychological pressure, despite Iran's ratification of international human rights instruments prohibiting torture and Iran's own laws forbidding "Any form of torture for the purpose of extracting confessions or gaining information" and making it impermissible "to compel individuals to give testimony, make confessions, or swear oaths" (Article 38 of the Constitution). Such confessions have consistently been treated as the sole evidence in a case and the basis for a conviction.

In its General Comment 13 (21) the Human Rights Committee stated that:

> "In order to safeguard the rights of the accused under

paragraphs 1 and 3 of Article 14, judges should have
authority to consider any allegations made of violations of
the rights of the accused during any stage of the
prosecution.''

Amnesty International knows of no cases in which the judge has
taken such matters as allegations of torture into consideration, or
has investigated their truth, or taken any kind of remedial or
compensatory measures.

4) Article 14, paragraph 4 states:

"In the case of juvenile persons the procedure shall be such
as will take account of their age and the desirability of
promoting their rehabilitation.''

In some cases Amnesty International is aware of preferential
conditions of imprisonment having been awarded to juveniles
imprisoned on political grounds. However, frequently juveniles and
adults accused in political cases have been treated no differently
either as regards the conditions in which they are held or the kind of
courts where they have been tried and the sentences passed. Indeed,
Amnesty International has gathered numerous testimonies of
former prisoners who have described the situation of juveniles held
on political grounds in their cells, among them some who were
subsequently executed.

5) Paragraph 5 of Article 14 provides that:

"Everyone convicted of a crime shall have the right to his
conviction and sentence being reviewed by a higher tribunal
according to law.''

In political cases the defendant has no right of appeal against
conviction and sentence and no right to seek a review of the
application of the law in his or her case through recourse to a court of
cassation. In almost all the cases Amnesty International knows
about the decision of the first court has been considered final. As
noted above, most political cases are tried by Islamic Revolutionary
Courts, and under Note 2 to Article 11 of the Administrative
Regulations Governing the Revolutionary Courts and Public
Prosecutors' Offices:

"Judgments of the Revolutionary Court shall be final and
no revision be made thereon.''

In 1983 the Supreme Judicial Council issued two circulars dealing
with the right of appeal against conviction and sentence. The first
declared that revision of court judgments was not permissible,

following the earlier stated view of the Guardians Council that:

> "Revision of the judgment of the *Shari'a* judge is not allowed except in instances of claim of non-competence of the judge by any one of the two parties to the case and in instances where the judgment is considered to be contradictory to the provisions of the *Fiqh* or omission by the judge of *ratio decidendi.*"

The second stated that, in accordance with the above-stated view of the Guardians Council, and in view of Article 4 of the Constitution, which provides that all laws and regulations should be based on Islamic criteria, all courts of appeal should be dissolved.

Amnesty International considers the need for appeal is the greater where courts presided over by a single judge, sitting *in camera*, pass summary judgments and impose death penalties on defendants denied legal representation and the right to call witnesses. These circumstances make illegalities and injustices during the trial more likely, and require review and supervision by higher courts.

Amnesty International is aware of the statement by the spokesman of the Supreme Judicial Council, Hojatoleslam Moqtadaie, in early 1986 that:

> "... whenever it may be deemed to be permissible by Islamic Jurisprudence to review and revise such verdicts [passed by Revolutionary Courts] then the same shall be referred, by invocation of the judgment pronounced by the Imam [Khomeini] to a higher court for reconsideration. In case the higher court after study of the file decides that judgment has not been duly passed, the said court will reverse the judgment and return the file for further investigation to the same court or a similar court. One bench of the Supreme Court has been allocated for this purpose."

Amnesty International welcomes the introduction of this measure as a first step towards introducing a clearly defined appeals procedure applicable to everyone convicted by any court in the Islamic Republic of Iran. Such a procedure should not prejudice the right to seek pardon or commutation of sentence.

6) Article 14 (6) provides that:

> "When a person has by a final decision been convicted of a criminal offence and when subsequently his conviction has been reversed or he has been pardoned on the ground that a new or newly discovered fact shows that there has been a miscarriage of justice, the person who has suffered punishment as a result of such conviction shall be compensated

according to law, unless it is proved that the non-disclosure of the unknown fact in time is wholly or partly attributable to him."

Amnesty International has no information about the reversal and pardoning of offences in the Islamic Republic of Iran in circumstances such as those described above, since in practice there is normally no procedure for such a review of conviction and sentence. In those instances brought to Amnesty International's attention in which there has clearly been a miscarriage of justice (such as the wrongful imprisonment or execution of someone whose name resembled that of a known political opposition activist) the organization is not aware of any procedure or measures having been followed or undertaken to compensate either the victim or his or her family.

7) Paragraph 7 of Article 14 of the Covenant states that:

"No one shall be liable to be tried or punished again for an offence for which he has already been finally convicted or acquitted in accordance with the law and penal procedure of each country."

Amnesty International has received information about a number of cases in which individuals were executed after having been tried and sentenced to terms of imprisonment on political grounds. It is not clear in most cases whether there were further judicial proceedings. This is obviously a breach of the above provision of the International Covenant on Civil and Political Rights.

The right of all political prisoners to a fair and prompt trial is a crucial part of Amnesty International's mandate; the organization therefore strongly recommends immediate steps to guarantee all political prisoners in the Islamic Republic of Iran fair trials. Consequently it suggests an urgent review of all stages in the judicial process in order to integrate in their entirety the important basic safeguards contained in Article 14 of the International Covenant on Civil and Political Rights. Amnesty International considers such measures the requisite minimum for working towards the guarantee of fair trials for all political prisoners.

Amnesty International realizes that the revised Penal Procedure Code has yet to be approved and fully implemented. It is also aware that the Islamic Penal Code of Iran too has yet to be finally approved following its five-year trial period. In view of this the organization is making the following recommendations, based on its understanding of legislation concerning courts and the administration of justice in the Islamic Republic of Iran and the relevant principles of international human rights law:

1. The law should be amended to include an independent judicial decision-making procedure, free of extrajudicial or executive influence.

2. The law should be amended to require that those who are appointed as judges shall have had appropriate training and be legally qualified.

3. The law should be amended to require non-discrimination in the selection of judges on the grounds of race, colour, sex, religion, political or other opinions, national or social origin, property, birth or status in accordance with Basic Principle 10 of the UN Basic Principles on the Independence of the Judiciary.

Finally, Amnesty International would draw attention to the Human Rights Committee's General Comment on the International Covenant on Civil and Political Rights 3 (13) that:

"(I)mplementation does not depend solely on constitutional or legislative enactments, which in themselves are often not *per se* sufficient. The Committee considers it necessary to draw the attention of States Parties to the fact that their obligation under the Covenant is not confined to the respect of human rights, but that States Parties have also undertaken to ensure the enjoyment of these rights to all individuals under their jurisdiction. This aspect calls for specific activities by the States Parties to enable individuals to enjoy their rights."

5. *The death penalty and executions*

Amnesty International unreservedly opposes the death penalty in all cases. It considers the penalty a violation of the right to life and the most extreme form of cruel, inhuman or degrading treatment or punishment. It therefore deeply regrets the thousands of death sentences passed and executions carried out in the Islamic Republic of Iran in recent years, including the execution of many individuals for their non-violent political or religious beliefs or activities.

The organization does not know the precise number of executions for each year, and regrets that its requests for official figures have not been answered. Although its own record of the number of executions is far from exhaustive, in the six months between July and December 1981 it recorded 2,444 executions. It recorded a total of 470 executions in 1985. It believes these figures are considerably lower than those for the actual number of executions. It believes that fewer executions are now taking place in the Islamic Republic of

Iran, however the most recent figures the organization has recorded show that a considerable number of Iranian citizens are losing their lives through judicial execution.

The Islamic Penal Code of Iran provides for the death penalty for numerous offences.[6] Judicial execution may be carried out by hanging, firing squad or stoning[7] and may take place in public, the body being left on view after the execution.

In the early 1980s Amnesty International gathered detailed information about mass executions and recorded a number of cases in which minors were executed in the Islamic Republic of Iran for political offences. Among the many former prisoners interviewed by the organization's representatives outside Iran was a young man who had himself been sentenced to death when aged 16 in a town in northern Iran, and had managed to escape from prison. In this case Amnesty International was able to verify the details of his testimony by interviewing another prisoner, a member of a different political group, who had been imprisoned with him. Neither was aware of Amnesty International's interview with the other. Amnesty International has also received many reports of the execution of juveniles, some as young as 11, in 1981 and 1982.

Amnesty International has received reports also of pregnant women being executed. This is contrary to Iran's Islamic Penal Code (*Hodoud* and *Qesas*), Article 106 of which states:

"While a woman is pregnant or in labour the punishment of killing or stoning to death is not inflicted on her, nor after childbirth if the newborn child does not have a supporter or it is feared that the baby would die; if there is a supporter the punishment should be inflicted on her."

Amnesty International, while opposing the application of the death penalty unconditionally, is even more concerned when death sentences are passed following trials which fail to meet internationally recognized standards. It believes that the death penalty has repeatedly been imposed in political cases following summary trials lasting a matter of minutes, in which the accused has had no access at any stage to legal counsel and has been denied both the right to appeal against conviction and sentence and to seek pardon or commutation of the sentence.

---

[6]These are listed in *Memorandum from Amnesty International to the Islamic Republic of Iran concerning the Islamic Penal Code of Iran* dated 8 August 1986 [see pages 63-64].

[7]Please refer to the *Memorandum from Amnesty International to the Islamic Republic of Iran concerning the Islamic Penal Code of Iran* dated 8 August 1986.

The Human Rights Committee concluded in General Comment 6 (16) on Article 6 of the Covenant:

"While it follows from Article 6 (2) to (6) that States parties are not obliged to abolish the death penalty totally, they are obliged to limit its use and, in particular, to abolish it for other than 'the most serious crimes'... The article also refers generally to abolition in terms which strongly suggest (paragraphs 2 (2) and (6)) that abolition is desirable...

"The Committee is of the opinion that the expression 'most serious crimes' must be read restrictively to mean that the death penalty should be *a quite exceptional measure*. It also follows from the express terms of Article 6 that it can only be imposed in accordance with the law in force at the time of the commission of the crime and not contrary to the Covenant. The procedural guarantees therein prescribed must be observed, including the right to a fair hearing by an independent tribunal, the presumption of innocence, the minimum guarantees for the defence, and the right to review by a higher tribunal. These rights are applicable in addition to the particular right to seek pardon or commutation of the sentence." (Emphasis added)

Article 119 of the Islamic Penal Code of Iran (*Hodoud* and *Qesas*) states:

"In the punishment of stoning to death, the stones should not be too large so that the person dies on being hit by one or two of them; they should not be so small either that they could not be defined as stones."[8]

This punishment has been and continues to be implemented. Amnesty International knows of four cases of individuals being sentenced to death and executed by stoning during the first half of 1986.

The organization urges the Government of the Islamic Republic of Iran to demonstrate its respect for the inherent right to life by immediately and finally abolishing executions. Pending the carrying out of such a decision, the organization would draw attention to United Nations Resolution 35/172, adopted by the General Assembly on 15 December 1980, urging all Member States:

"1. (a) To respect *as a minimum standard* the content of the

---

[8]Offences punishable by stoning to death (*rajm*) are listed in the *Memorandum from Amnesty International to the Islamic Republic of Iran concerning the Islamic Penal Code of Iran* dated 8 August 1986 [see page 63].

provisions of articles 6, 14 and 15 of the International
Covenant on Civil and Political Rights and, where necessary, to review their legal rules and practices so as to
guarantee the most careful legal procedures and the greatest
possible safeguards for the accused in capital cases;
[emphasis added]

(b) To examine the possibility of making automatic the
appeal procedure, where it exists, in cases of death
sentences, as well as the consideration of an amnesty,
pardon or commutation in these cases;

(c) To provide that no death sentence shall be carried out
until the procedures of appeal and pardon have been
terminated and, in any case, not until a reasonable time after
the passing of the sentence in the court in the first instance."

Amnesty International would also draw attention to Resolution
32/61 adopted by the United Nations General Assembly on 8
December 1977 which, among other things, reaffirmed that:

"... the main objective to be pursued in the field of capital
punishment is that of progressively restricting the number of
offences for which the death penalty may be imposed with a
view to the desirability of abolishing this punishment..."

6. Other judicial punishments of concern to Amnesty International

Amnesty International is disturbed by the continuing provision, in
the Islamic Republic of Iran, for such punishments as the
amputation of limbs or fingers, flogging and crucifixion. The
provisions in the Islamic Penal Code of Iran prescribing such
punishments are noted in the *Memorandum from Amnesty International to the Islamic Republic of Iran concerning the Islamic Penal
Code of Iran.*

Amnesty International is concerned too about reports of the
summary nature of criminal trial proceedings in such cases. It
believes that the infliction of such punishments, which it considers
forms of cruel, inhuman or degrading treatment or punishment, is
an even graver matter when basic legal safeguards are absent. It has,
for example, received reports of flogging sentences being carried out
immediately after sentencing, with no right to appeal against
conviction or sentence, often following a summary trial.

The reports of flogging received by Amnesty International have
not mentioned any medical examination either before or after the
infliction of the prescribed number of lashes, and it has received

reports of women who, having been flogged when pregnant, have subsequently had miscarriages. This is evidently a breach of Article 107 of the Islamic Penal Code of Iran (*Hodoud* and *Qesas*) which states:

> "If the infliction of whipping is likely to harm the foetus or suckling baby, the whipping of a pregnant or nursing woman should be delayed."

The Penal Code gives some indication about how flogging should be inflicted. According to Article 115 the punishment for fornication is prescribed thus:

> "A man, while standing and his body naked except for a cover on his private parts, is whipped all over the body except on his head, face and private parts. A woman, however, is whipped while sitting with her dress tied to her body."

The same manner of enforcement, according to Article 132, is inflicted on those convicted of drinking alcohol.

In cases of *qazf* (malicious accusation), however, which is also punishable by flogging, "Whips are applied over the normal dress with medium force, not as in whipping for fornication" (Article 187). A note to this article adds that the head, face and private parts of the convicted person should not be whipped.

Amnesty International has interviewed both a number of former prisoners who were themselves flogged as a judicial punishment and many others apparently flogged in order to extract information or confessions. (See Section 3.) From these interviews the organization has concluded that flogging methods have been harsher than those prescribed by law. Although some victims have claimed that the lashes were delivered with minimal force, others have told Amnesty International that they were lashed very hard by several officers in turn, and that the pain was so intense that they lost consciousness. Indeed, Amnesty International knows of cases in which the physical results of such lashings lasted for many months; in some cases prolonged medical treatment has been necessary because of damage to internal organs.

The Islamic Penal Code of Iran, in stipulating a number of offences that are punishable by amputation, also prescribes the manner in which this should be inflicted. Article 218 (*Hodoud* and *Qesas*) states:

> "*Hadd* for theft for the first time is the dismembering of four fingers of the right hand of the thief from the fingers' extremity so that only the thumb and palm of the thief

remain; for the second time the dismembering of the left foot of the thief from the lower part of the protrusion so that half his foot and part of the place of anointment remain; for the third time the thief is condemned to life imprisonment; for the fourth time, if he commits theft in the prison, he shall be condemned to death.

"Note 1: A number of thefts, so long as the *hadd* is not inflicted, shall be regarded as one theft.

"Note 2: Where the fingers of the thief's hand are dismembered and after the infliction of this punishment another theft committed by him prior to the infliction of the punishment is proved, his left foot shall be dismembered."

Amnesty International does not have a complete record of the number of amputations carried out. However, during 1985 and the first half of 1986, it recorded 11 cases (all of which were reported in Iranian newspapers) involving individuals convicted of repeated theft.

In an interview published by *Keyhan International* on 16 February 1986, Hojatoleslam Moqtadaie, spokesman of the Supreme Judicial Council, stated that there had been "numerous cases of severing of hands in Tehran and other provincial cities".

Amputations are believed at the moment to be inflicted by the Judicial Police. According to an interview reported in *Keyhan* on 21 November 1984, the head of the Judicial Police, Abbas Hashemi Ishaqpour, said:

"The Judicial Police have already prepared a device which very speedily severs the hand of the thief... To facilitate the enactment of Islamic law on severance of thieves' hands, help has been sought from relevant competent authorities, such as the Coroner's Office, the Ministry of Health, and the Medical Faculties of Tehran and Beheshti Universities."

The machine was reportedly installed in February 1985 in Qasr Prison and, Amnesty International believes, is still being used to amputate fingers.

Article 202 of the Islamic Penal Code of Iran (*Hodoud* and *Qesas*) permits hanging with gallows as one of four alternative punishments for the *mohareb* and *mofsed fil arz*. Article 207 lays down the following conditions for the infliction of this punishment, which would appear to constitute crucifixion:

"a) The manner of tying does not cause his death.

b) He does not remain on the cross for more than three days; but if he dies during the three days, he may be brought down after his death.

c) If he remains alive after three days, he must not be killed.''

Amnesty International considers that all the above-mentioned punishments are forms of cruel, inhuman or degrading treatment or punishment and, as such, should be replaced with penalties which are compatible with international human rights standards.

As regards flogging, Amnesty International respectfully draws the attention of the Government of the Islamic Republic of Iran to the Human Rights Committee's General Comment 7 (16) which states: "... the prohibition [of torture and other cruel, inhuman or degrading treatment or punishment] must extend to corporal punishment, including excessive chastisement as an educational or disciplinary measure.''

As for amputation, Amnesty International recalls that in August 1984 the United Nations Sub-Commission on Prevention of Discrimination and Protection of Minorities adopted a resolution (1984/22) recommending the United Nations Commission on Human Rights to urge governments which had legislation providing for the penalty of amputation to prescribe different punishments in accordance with Article 5 of the Universal Declaration of Human Rights which prohibits "cruel, inhuman or degrading treatment or punishment''.

Amnesty International respectfully submits that all the above-mentioned punishments do not meet recognized international standards for the prevention and punishment of crime and treatment of offenders and contravene Article 38 of the Constitution of the Islamic Republic of Iran, which forbids the use of torture, and Article 39 which forbids: "All affronts to the dignity and honour of persons arrested, detained, imprisoned, or banished in accordance with the law...'' and urges that they be promptly replaced.

7. Summary and recommendations

Amnesty International's concern about the arrest, detention and treatment of political prisoners, as well as about judicial punishments, is described in some detail in Sections 3 to 6. The following, however, is a brief summary of the organization's conclusions with regard to the above matters of concern and its recommendations to the Government of the Islamic Republic of Iran.

A. Political arrest and imprisonment [9]

A.1 Amnesty International knows that many individuals are currently imprisoned in the Islamic Republic of Iran who would fall within the organization's definition of a prisoner of conscience. (Men and women imprisoned because of their political, religious or other conscientiously held beliefs, or by reason of their ethnic origin, sex, colour or language, who have neither used nor advocated violence.)

Amnesty International acknowledges that some prisoners of conscience have benefited from amnesties or reduction of prison sentences, but believes that no individual should be imprisoned for the non-violent expression of his or her conscientiously held beliefs, or for the other reasons described above. It therefore calls for the immediate and unconditional release of all prisoners of conscience in the Islamic Republic of Iran.

A.2 In view of the wealth of evidence available about the conduct of law enforcement agencies when arresting individuals falling within Amnesty International's terms of reference, particularly with regard to the excessive use of force, and the subsequent ill-treatment of those detained, Amnesty International respectfully recommends an urgent and thorough review of training procedures provided for all law enforcement agencies in the Islamic Republic of Iran. Such training should take into account the directives laid down in the United Nations Code of Conduct for Law Enforcement Officials (adopted by the United Nations General Assembly on 17 December 1979).

A.3 There has been frequent arbitrary arrest and detention of political suspects and/or their families. Amnesty International respectfully urges the introduction and carrying out of procedural legislation to ensure protection from arbitrary arrest in accordance with Article 9 (1) and (2) of the International Covenant on Civil and Political Rights and Article 32 of the Constitution of the Islamic Republic of Iran, which states:

"No one can be arrested except in accordance with judgment and procedure established by law. In the case of arrest, charges and supporting evidence must be communicated immediately in writing and be elucidated to him..."

A.4 According to Amnesty International's information arrests in connection with suspected political activities are often made in

---

[9]Please also refer to Recommendations 4 and 5 in the *Memorandum from Amnesty International to the Islamic Republic of Iran concerning the Islamic Penal Code of Iran* dated 8 August 1986 [see pages 68 and 69].

50

circumstances which do not permit the relatives of the arrested
person to be informed either of the arrest or of the person's
subsequent whereabouts. Amnesty International respectfully draws
the attention of the Government of the Islamic Republic of Iran to
Rule 92 of the United Nations Standard Minimum Rules for the
Treatment of Prisoners (adopted by the First United Nations
Congress on the Prevention of Crime and the Treatment of
Offenders, held in Geneva in 1955, and approved by the Economic
and Social Council by its resolutions 663C (XXIV) of 31 July 1957
and 2076 (LXII) of 13 May 1977), which states:

> "An untried prisoner shall be allowed to inform immediately
> his family of his detention and shall be given all reasonable
> facilities for communicating with his family and friends, and
> for receiving visits from them, subject only to such
> restrictions and supervision as are necessary in the interests
> of the administration of justice and of the security and good
> order of the institution."

A.5   Amnesty International is disturbed by reports, which it is still
receiving, that relatives of suspected political activists have been
arrested and detained and, on occasion, sentenced to terms of
imprisonment, in cases in which the alleged offender has not been
found and in which those actually detained have not engaged in the
activity in question. Amnesty International respectfully points out
that it is a principle common to all legal systems that persons should
not be punished for offences they have not committed, and urges
that this be discontinued.

B.   Torture and ill-treatment[10]

B.1   Amnesty International is disturbed by reports that torture and
cruel, inhuman or degrading treatment or punishment of prisoners
continues to take place in the Islamic Republic of Iran. Amnesty
International recognizes that torture is forbidden in the Constitution
of the Islamic Republic of Iran "... for the purpose of extracting
confessions or gaining information" and that the infliction or
ordering of ill-treatment of prisoners is a punishable offence under
Iranian law. Nevertheless, Amnesty International considers that
further measures are urgently needed to ensure that torture and ill-
treatment of prisoners does not occur. Such measures should, in

---

[10]Please also refer to Recommendations 2 and 3 in the *Memorandum from Amnesty International to the Islamic Republic of Iran concerning the Islamic Penal Code of Iran* dated 8 August 1986 [see page 68].

general, include the following:

(a) clear and publicized condemnation of the use of torture should be made by the highest authorities in the land;

(b) all detainees should be held in publicly recognized places of detention or prisons, and not in secret places;

(c) legislation prohibiting torture should be strengthened to include an unequivocal prohibition of torture in the Constitution and should be seen to be carried out;

(d) those responsible for inflicting or ordering the use of torture should be brought to justice;

(e) the training of all law enforcement agencies should emphasize the total prohibition of the use of torture;

(f) victims of torture should be compensated.

B.2 Amnesty International is concerned about the lack of basic safeguards in the treatment of political detainees. It respectfully recommends that the following steps be taken without delay:

(a) a legal limit should be prescribed and strictly enforced to restrict incommunicado detention; in Amnesty International's experience, prolonged incommunicado detention is frequently conducive to torture and ill-treatment;

(b) anyone arrested or detained should have the right to challenge his or her detention before a judicial authority, in accordance with Article 9 (3) of the International Covenant on Civil and Political Rights. In the opinion of the Human Rights Committee the delay between arrest and such procedure "must not exceed a few days" (General Comment 8 (16));

(c) there should be a set limit to solitary confinement, which the Human Rights Committee has held "may, according to the circumstances, and especially when the person is kept incommunicado, be contrary to... [Article 7 of the International Covenant on Civil and Political Rights]" which forbids the use of torture (General Comment 7 (16));

(d) that, in addition to being permitted family visits, as mentioned above, all detainees should be granted, in all cases, prompt and regular access to legal counsel of their own choosing, as well as to qualified medical personnel when necessary.

B.3 Amnesty International knows of numerous allegations of torture and ill-treatment, both physical and psychological, of prisoners in the Islamic Republic of Iran. The organization respectfully urges that a public and impartial investigation be conducted into allegations of torture and ill-treatment, and that there should be a thorough review of the administrative and judicial procedures regulating the arrest, confinement and interrogation of political suspects. The inquiry's findings and its working methods should be made public.

Pending the establishment of such a commission, its findings and recommendations, Amnesty International recommends the immediate establishment of basic, practical safeguards. These should include:

(a) clear notification to the next of kin that someone has been arrested plus clear indication of his or her whereabouts;

(b) access for each detainee to relatives and a lawyer of his or her own choosing, both immediately after arrest and at brief, regular intervals thereafter;

(c) each detainee should be examined by a qualified doctor on arrival in prison and periodically thereafter; a copy of the medical report (fully respecting the confidentiality of its contents) should be kept by a central authority;

(d) frequent and unannounced visits should be made by people independent of the authorities responsible for detaining, investigating or prosecuting the prisoners. The purpose of this should be to inspect all prisons and detention centres to record and seek redress for prisoners' complaints and to monitor standards of medical treatment, food and hygiene; copies of these reports should be kept and monitored by a central authority.

B.4   On 10 December 1984 the United Nations General Assembly adopted the Convention against Torture and Other Cruel, Inhuman or Degrading Treatment or Punishment, through Resolution 39/46, which called upon "... all Governments to consider signing and ratifying the Convention as a matter of priority." The Convention obliges all States Parties to it to make torture a punishable offence and to prevent the use of torture in their jurisdictions. Amnesty International respectfully urges the Government of the Islamic Republic of Iran to take immediate steps to become a party to the Convention against Torture, which has so far been acceded to or ratified by 10 states and signed by 47 others.[11]

---

[11]As of 1 November 1986.

C. Unfair trial [12]

C.1 Amnesty International is disturbed by the numerous and consistent reports of summary trials of political prisoners, particularly those trials taking place before Islamic Revolutionary Courts. The organization respectfully recommends an urgent review of all stages of the judicial process in order to integrate into them all the basic safeguards established in Article 14 of the International Covenant on Civil and Political Rights. Amnesty International considers such a measure would be an important step towards the protection of prisoners from summary and unfair trials.

Amnesty International therefore respectfully draws the attention of the Government of the Islamic Republic of Iran to General Comment 3(21) by the Human Rights Committee on Article 14 of the International Covenant on Civil and Political Rights, which notes the existence in many countries of military or special courts which try civilians, but indicates that such proceedings "should be very exceptional and take place under conditions which genuinely afford the full guarantees stipulated in Article 14".

Amnesty International is deeply concerned about the conduct of trials before Islamic Revolutionary Courts. It considers that the Administrative Regulations Governing Revolutionary Courts and Public Prosecutors Offices contain inadequate provisions to ensure fair trials, and it is Amnesty International's experience that even safeguards established by law are not maintained. Amnesty International understands that these courts were created as a temporary measure only and recommends that consideration now be given to abolishing them so as to consolidate all judicial proceedings in one system, which should supply all the safeguards necessary for a fair trial. Amnesty International respectfully recommends that such steps be taken into consideration in the course of making any review of existing legislation.

C.2 Amnesty International understands that the revised Penal Procedure Code has yet to be approved in its entirety. It understands too that the Islamic Penal Code of Iran has yet to be finally approved following a five-year trial period. In view of this the organization respectfully recommends that the legislative provisions be amended:

(a) to permit an independent judicial decision-making process free of extra-legal or executive influence;

---

[12]Please refer also to Recommendations 2, 3, 7, 8, 9 and 10 in the *Memorandum from Amnesty International to the Islamic Republic of Iran concerning the Islamic Penal Code of Iran* dated 8 August 1986 [see pages 68 and 69].

54

    (b) to require that those appointed as judges shall have the appropriate legal training and qualifications;

    (c) to ensure non-discrimination in the selection of judges on the grounds of race, colour, sex, religion, political or other opinions, or social origin, in accordance with Basic Principle 10 of the Basic Principles on the Independence of the Judiciary, adopted by the Seventh United Nations Congress on the Prevention of Crime and Treatment of Offenders in September 1985 and endorsed by the United Nations General Assembly in Resolution 40/32 of 29 November 1985.

C.3   Finally, in recommending that all provisions of Article 14 of the International Covenant on Civil and Political Rights be legally enforced without delay, as a minimum step towards protection from unfair trial Amnesty International respectfully recalls the Human Rights Committee's General Comment 3(13) on the implementation of the Covenant:

> "Implementation does not depend solely on constitutional or legislative enactments, which in themselves are often not *per se* sufficient. The Committee considers it necessary to draw the attention of States Parties to the fact that their obligation under the Covenant is not confined to the respect of human rights, but that States Parties have also undertaken to ensure the enjoyment of these rights to all individuals under their jurisdiction. This aspect calls for specific activities by the States parties to enable individuals to enjoy their rights."

D. *The death penalty*[13]

D.1 Amnesty International annually records numerous executions in the Islamic Republic of Iran, often carried out after summary trials, and the victims not having been accorded the right to appeal against conviction and sentence.

Amnesty International respectfully urges the Government of the Islamic Republic of Iran to demonstrate its respect for the inherent right to life by putting an immediate end to executions.

Pending the carrying out of such a decision, Amnesty International would draw the attention of the Government of the Islamic Republic of Iran to Resolution 35/172 adopted by the United

---

[13]Please also refer to Recommendation 6 in the *Memorandum from Amnesty International to the Islamic Republic of Iran concerning the Islamic Penal Code of Iran* dated 8 August 1986 [see page 69].

Nations General Assembly on 15 December 1980, which urged all Member States:

> "1 (a) To respect as a minimum standard the contents of the provisions of articles 6, 14 and 15 of the International Covenant on Civil and Political Rights and, where necessary, to review their legal rules and practices so as to guarantee the most careful legal procedures and the greatest possible safeguards for the accused in capital cases;
>
> (b) To examine carefully the possibility of making automatic the appeal procedure, where it exists, in cases of death sentences, as well as the consideration of an amnesty, pardon or commutation in these cases;
>
> (c) To provide that no death sentence shall be carried out until the procedures of appeal and pardon have been terminated and, in any case, not until a reasonable time after passing of the sentence in the court in the first instance."

E. Other judicial punishments of concern to Amnesty International [14]

E.1 Amnesty International is concerned about the legal provision for, and in some cases continuing application of, judicial punishments which are incompatible with Article 7 of the International Covenant on Civil and Political Rights, which prohibits the use of torture, or cruel, inhuman or degrading treatment or punishment. Such punishments include stoning to death and crucifixion, as well as flogging and amputation of fingers or limbs, including cross-limb amputation. Amnesty International respectfully recommends the replacement of such punishments by other penalties which are consistent with recognized international standards for the prevention and punishment of crime and the treatment of offenders.

---

[14]Please refer also to Recommendation 1 in the *Memorandum from Amnesty International to the Islamic Republic of Iran concerning the Islamic Penal Code of Iran* dated 8 August 1986 [see page 68].

Memorandum from Amnesty International to the Islamic Republic of Iran concerning the Islamic Penal Code of Iran

(8 August 1986)

1. Introduction

This memorandum reviews the Islamic Penal Code of Iran[1], including the Law of *Hodoud* and *Qesas* and the *Ta'azirat*, which contains provisions that concern Amnesty International. The memorandum makes no reference to *Diyat*, whose provisions do not fall within Amnesty International's terms of reference. The Law of *Hodoud* and *Qesas* was provisionally adopted for a trial period of five years in 1982 (Iranian calendar 1361), within the context of the Constitution of the Islamic Republic of Iran adopted in 1979 (1358). The *Ta'azirat* were approved in 1983 (1362) on a trial basis for five years.

This analysis indicates provisions in the Islamic Penal Code of Iran which concern Amnesty International and should be considered for revision in the light of international human rights and humanitarian law standards. Amnesty International's principal concerns are torture, the imprisonment of individuals, who have not used or advocated violence, on account of their conscientiously held beliefs (prisoners of conscience), the death penalty, and unfair trials in political cases.

While every effort has been made to present an accurate interpretation of the legislation, Amnesty International would welcome clarification of any areas where it is felt that accuracy has not been achieved. Indeed, Amnesty International is prepared to send a delegation to the Islamic Republic of Iran to discuss this document with the appropriate authorities.

Amnesty International of course recognizes the legitimacy of penal codes formulated according to a country's social, cultural, religious, and other traditions. The organization also notes that provisions of the Islamic Penal Code of Iran reflect *Shari'a*.

---

[1]The articles cited herein refer to the texts published in Official Gazettes Nos. 10972, 10987, 10988 and 11278.

However, when such laws risk violating international human rights law, Amnesty International is constrained to point out these breaches. The Islamic Republic of Iran is a party to the International Covenant on Civil and Political Rights and has continued to submit reports to the Human Rights Committee, thereby demonstrating its intention to be bound by this principal human rights instrument. The International Covenant on Civil and Political Rights was adopted unanimously by the UN General Assembly and has been ratified by more than 80 countries with a wide variety of legal systems.

The following analysis, consequently, will focus on Amnesty International's statutory human rights concerns as they relate to specific articles in the Islamic Penal Code of Iran which, in their present form, appear to be incompatible with the International Covenant on Civil and Political Rights as well as other international human rights standards.

2. Torture

The Universal Declaration of Human Rights (Article 5), the International Covenant on Civil and Political Rights (Article 7) and several other international human rights instruments forbid torture or cruel, inhuman or degrading treatment or punishment.

Article 38 of the Constitution of the Islamic Republic of Iran is consistent with these international norms in specifying:

"Any form of torture for the purpose of extracting confessions or gaining information is forbidden. It is not permissible to compel individuals to give testimony, make confessions, or swear oaths, and any testimony, confession, or oath obtained in this fashion is worthless and invalid. Punishments for the infringement of these principles will be determined by law."

There are a few provisions in the Islamic Penal Code of Iran which would appear to forbid torture: for example, Article 58 of the *Ta'azirat* forbids physical ill-treatment in order to obtain a confession, thus rendering the infliction or ordering of such acts punishable offences. Similarly, Article 49 of the Law of *Hodoud* and *Qesas* states: "Retribution by a blunt and unsharp instrument causing torment to the criminal is not permitted."

The Islamic Penal Code of Iran, however, contains several provisions which impose punishments constituting torture or cruel, inhuman, or degrading treatment or punishment. The punishments include stoning, crucifixion, mutilation and flogging.

A. *Stoning*

Article 119 of the Law of *Hodoud* and *Qesas* makes clear that the purpose of stoning is the intentional infliction of grievous pain leading to death. Article 119 states with respect to the penalty for adultery:

"In the punishment of stoning to death, the stones should not be too large so that the person dies on being hit by one or two of them; they should not be so small either that they could not be defined as stones."

B. *Crucifixion*

Article 207 of the Law of *Hodoud* and *Qesas* also makes clear that the purpose of crucifixion is the intentional infliction of severe pain or suffering which may lead to death. Article 207 states:

"The crucifixion of a *mohareb* [at enmity with God] and *mofsed fil arz* [corrupt on earth] shall be carried out by observing the following conditions:

a) The manner of tying does not cause his death;

b) He does not remain on the cross for more than three days; but if he dies during the period of three days, he may be brought down after his death;

c) If he remains alive after three days, he must not be killed."

C. *Mutilation*

The Law of *Hodoud* and *Qesas* contains provisions calling for amputation of limbs and mutilation of other parts of the body for such offences as being *mohareb* and *mofsed fil arz* under Article 208, theft under Article 218 and intentional mayhem or inflicting injury to a limb under Articles 55-80. Article 218, for example, provides:

"Punishment of *hadd* for theft for the first time is the dismembering of four fingers of the right hand of the thief from the fingers' extremity so that the thumb and palm of the thief remain; for the second time, the dismembering of the left foot of the thief from the lower part of the protrusion so that half his foot and part of the place of anointing remain; for the third time the thief is condemned to imprisonment for life; for the fourth time, if he commits theft in the prison, he shall be condemned to death."

Amputation and mutilation constitute a form of cruel, inhuman, or degrading punishment, which is specifically prohibited under international law. Even during periods of armed conflict, the Geneva Convention relative to the Protection of Civilian Persons in

Time of War, to which the Islamic Republic of Iran is a party, forbids "violence to life and person, in particular murder of all kinds, *mutilation*, cruel treatment and torture" (common Article 3, emphasis added; see also Article 32). The United Nations Sub-Commission on Prevention of Discrimination and Protection of Minorities in its Resolution 1984/22 noted "the existence in various countries of legislation or practices providing for the penalty of amputation"; recalled Article 5 of the Universal Declaration of Human Rights which forbids torture or cruel, inhuman or degrading punishment; and recommended to the Commission on Human Rights to urge governments which have such legislation or practices to take appropriate measures to prescribe different punishment consistent with Article 5. (UN Doc. E/CN.4/1985/3, at 95 (1986))

D. *Flogging*

The Law of *Hodoud* and *Qesas* contains a number of provisions prescribing flogging for those who commit such offences as adultery (Articles 100-104), taking alcohol (Articles 123-136), sodomy (Article 152), lesbianism (Articles 159, 164), pimping (Article 168), and *qazf* (malicious accusation) (Articles 176, 178, 187). Article 102, for example, provides, "Punishment for fornication by a man or woman who is not qualified as married is one hundred (100) lashes." Article 178 prescribes flogging for a "discerning" minor who maliciously accuses someone. Article 131 provides, "Punishment for drinking liquor is eighty (80) lashes, whether it is a man or woman." Article 132 provides, "A man is whipped while standing with his body naked except for a cover on his private parts, but a woman is whipped while sitting with her dress tied to her body." (See the similar provisions in Article 115 for adultery). While Article 187 slightly ameliorates the kind of flogging imposed for malicious accusation, that provision gives some indication of the intention to inflict severe pain and suffering by flogging: "Lashes are inflicted over the normal clothes and with average force, not with the force used in the punishment for fornication."

The *Ta'azirat* provisions of the Islamic Penal Code of Iran contain more than 50 articles prescribing lashing of up to 74 strokes. The provisions include Articles: 29 (forgery), 37 (escape from prison), 38 (guard who negligently permits escape), 40 (negligent failure of an officer to arrest an accused person), 43 (assisting a criminal to elude justice), 45 (misuse of police or military uniform), 62 (an officer ordering or inflicting injury), 63 and 65 (government employee receiving a bribe), 64 (eavesdropping), 71 (unauthorized arresting or assisting in a "disappearance"), 72 (impersonating a government official), 76 and 80 (misuse of government funds),

78 (illegal collection of property by a government official), 82 (destruction of officially held documents), 87 (insulting high government officials), 88 (collusion in the commission of crimes against foreign or internal security), 89 (destruction of evidence or obstruction of justice), 97, 98 (refusal to return a child), 99 (abandonment of a child), 100 (tampering with a grave), 102 (failure of women to wear veils[2] and other offences in public places), 103 (encouraging prostitution), 105 (failure to support wife), 106 (medical personnel revealing patient's secrets), 107 (perjury), 108 (petty theft), 109 (attempted theft), 110 (receiving stolen property), 111 and 135 (trespass on land), 113 (threats to life, honour, or reputation), 115 (fraudulent bankruptcy), 116 (fraud), 117 (defrauding a minor), 118 (misuse of an official seal), 119 (failure to return property), 120-122 (other business fraud and deception including trade mark infringement), 127 (arson of building materials), 129 and 133 (destruction of property), 134, 135 (trespass on agricultural land), 137 (breaking and entering), 140, 141 and 143 (defamation), 145 (transactions involving alcohol), 146, 147 (establishment of and keeping a place for gambling or alcohol), 156 (driving without a licence), and 158 (tampering with a speedometer). There are a few other *Ta'azirat* provisions which carry the penalty of lashing: Article 86 (up to 30 lashes for vulgar insults) and Article 101 (up to 99 strokes for kissing by an unmarried couple).

Flogging or whipping constitute a form of torture or cruel, inhuman, or degrading treatment or punishment, specifically prohibited under international law. The Human Rights Committee has provided an authoritative interpretation of Article 7 of the International Covenant on Civil and Political Rights which prohibits torture or cruel, inhuman, or degrading treatment or punishment. Its general comment 7 (16) states:

"As appears from the terms of this article, the scope of protection required goes far beyond torture as normally understood. It may not be necessary to draw sharp distinctions between the various prohibited forms of treatment or punishment. These distinctions depend on the kind, purpose and severity of the particular treatment. In the view of the Committee *the prohibition must extend to corporal punishment*, including excessive chastisement as an educational or disciplinary measure..." UN Doc. A/37/40, at 94-95 (1986) (emphasis added)

---

[2] Prescribed dress for women in the Islamic Republic of Iran requires that all parts of the body, with the exception of face and hands, be completely concealed.

Even in periods of international armed conflict, the Geneva Convention relative to the Protection of Civilian Persons in Time of War prohibits:

"... any measure of such a character as to cause the physical suffering or extermination of protected persons... This prohibition applies not only to murder, torture, *corporal punishments, mutilation* and medical or scientific experiments..." (Article 32, emphasis added)

E. *Risk of torture through the need for confessions*

While the Constitution of the Islamic Republic of Iran forbids torture to obtain confessions, there are several provisions in the Law of *Hodoud* and *Qesas* which emphasize the use of confessions as a way of proving criminal guilt and which may encourage officials to use torture or other forms of duress to obtain such confessions. For example, Article 34 of the Law of *Hodoud* and *Qesas* states that if a person accused of murder "confesses to intention, he shall be subject to retribution. If he denies a premeditated murder and takes an oath [to this effect], he shall not be liable to retribution." Similarly, Article 85 provides a heavier punishment for those who confess on four occasions to fornication than for those who confess less often. Under Article 126 whipping is the penalty for a person who confesses twice to drinking wine. Article 145 provides, "By confessing four times to having committed sodomy, punishment is imposed on the one making the confession." Similarly, under Article 184, "*Qazf* [malicious accusation] is proved by two confessions." Such provisions would tend to encourage the law enforcement authorities to press accused individuals to confess. Such provisions requiring confessions create an extremely grave risk of torture being inflicted, despite formal bans on torture such as those found in Article 38 of the Constitution of the Islamic Republic of Iran.

There are also a number of other provisions in the Law of *Hodoud* and *Qesas* which make confession one of the principal means by which a criminal charge may be proved. For example, Article 27 explains the methods "by which a murder is proved in court" as follows: "1. Confession 2. Testimony 3. *Qassameh* [oath] 4. Knowledge of the judge"; Article 28: "By confessing to a premeditated murder, even if such a confession is made only once, a premeditated murder is proved"; Article 29: "A confession shall be effective and binding if the confessor meets the following conditions: has 1. a discerning mind 2. maturity 3. free will 4. intention. Therefore, the confession made by a lunatic, a drunkard, a child, someone under duress and those who lack will...

shall not be valid and binding.''

Analogous provisions in the Law of *Hodoud* and *Qesas* can be found in Articles 85-89 on fornication, Articles 126-127 on drinking alcohol, Articles 145-147 on sodomy, Articles 184-185 on malicious accusation, Article 201 on enmity towards God, and Article 216 on theft.

Indeed, a confession or a statement of repentance plays a significant part in the Law of *Hodoud* and *Qesas*. Article 138 provides that if ''someone repents after confessing to having taken liquor, the judge may either pardon him or impose punishment on him''. Article 162 provides, ''if a lesbian repents before the giving of testimony by the witnesses, the punishment will be quashed; if she does so after the giving of testimony, the punishment will not be quashed''.

While most of these provisions do not require confessions, as alternative means of proof are available through the use of witnesses and these provisions indicate that confessions shall be made freely, the emphasis the Law of *Hodoud* and *Qesas* gives to confessions may well tend to encourage law enforcement officials to press for confessions. In Amnesty International's experience this emphasis on confessions may provide an incentive for law enforcement officials to inflict torture.

The Islamic Penal Code of Iran does not appear to contain adequate safeguards to ensure the broad prohibition of torture set forth in Article 38 of the Constitution of the Islamic Republic of Iran. There are several measures which should be introduced, either in the revised Penal Code or in the Penal Procedure Code at present being considered, to help ensure that confessions are not made under duress or torture. First, all prisoners should be brought before a judicial authority promptly after being taken into custody, and relatives, lawyers, and doctors should have prompt and regular access to them. Second, prisoners should promptly be informed of their rights, including the right to lodge complaints about their treatment. There should be regular, independent visits of inspection to places of detention. There should be separation of the authorities responsible for detention from those in charge of interrogation. Third, all complaints and reports of torture should be impartially and thoroughly investigated, the methods and findings of such investigations being made public. Complainants and witnesses should be protected from intimidation. Fourth, there should be adequate means of challenging the use of confessions in criminal proceedings where such confessions or other evidence have been obtained through torture. Fifth, prosecutors should be encouraged to rely less upon confessions and more upon testimony by witnesses or other forms of evidence.

3. *Prisoners of conscience*

Amnesty International works for the unconditional release of all prisoners of conscience, that is, those who have been detained because of their race, religion, politics, language, beliefs, sex or for similar reasons, and have neither used nor advocated violence. According to Amnesty International's reading of the Islamic Penal Code of Iran, it does not contain provisions which would, if applied, result unequivocally in the incarceration of prisoners of conscience. This memorandum makes no attempt to comment on the present application of the Penal Code, but is obliged to indicate the existence of provisions which could be interpreted ambiguously. Amnesty International would recommend that any revision of the Penal Code should ensure the protection from incarceration of prisoners of conscience, and that legislation concerned with offences against the government or internal security is applied only to those using or advocating violence.

4. *The death penalty*

Amnesty International opposes the death penalty in all circumstances because it is a violation of the right to life and because it constitutes the ultimate form of cruel, inhuman, and degrading punishment.

The Law of *Hodoud* and *Qesas* prescribes the death penalty for a wide variety of offences, among them premeditated murder (Article 43); incest (Article 99 (a)); fornication with father's wife (Article 99 (b)); fornication by a non-Muslim with a Muslim woman (Article 99 (c)); fornication by force and coercion (Article 99 (d)); adultery by a married man (Article 100 (a), stoning to death) ; adultery by a married woman with an adult male (Article 100 (b), stoning to death); fornication for the fourth time by an unmarried person, having been punished for each previous offence (Article 105); drinking liquor for the third time, have been punished for each previous offence (Article 135); sodomy (Article 140); sexual intercourse by an adult male with an immature person (Article 143, adult male to be executed); *tafhiz* (homosexual conduct, without penetration) for the fourth time, having been punished for each previous offence (Article 153); lesbianism for the fourth time, having been punished for each previous offence (Article 161); malicious accusation for the fourth time, having been punished for each previous offence (Article 188); drawing arms to create fear and intimidation and destroy the freedom and security of the people (Articles 196, 202); armed robbery (Articles 197, 202); membership of or support for an organization which rises up in arms against the Islamic Government (Articles 198, 202); plotting to overthrow the Islamic Government and procuring arms for this purpose (Articles 199, 202); plotting to overthrow the Islamic Government and nominating oneself for a position in the post-coup government (Articles 200, 202).

While Amnesty International opposes the imposition of the death penalty in all circumstances, several of the death penalty provisions in the Law of *Hodoud* and *Qesas* do not conform with particular international human rights standards. Article 6 (2) of the International Covenant on Civil and Political Rights states: "In countries which have not abolished the death penalty, sentence of death may be imposed only for the most serious crimes in accordance with the law in force at the time of the commission of the crime..." Many of the offences for which the Law of *Hodoud* and *Qesas* prescribes the death penalty do not involve murder or serious bodily harm constituting the "most serious crimes", hence imposing the death penalty for these less serious crimes would be incompatible with the terms of Article 6 of the Covenant.

In addition, Article 6 (4) states: "Anyone sentenced to death shall have the right to seek pardon or commutation of the sentence..." There is no provision in the Law of *Hodoud* and *Qesas* for such pardon or commutation. Indeed, several articles in this Law would appear to make pardon or commutation more difficult, if not practically impossible to achieve. Articles 43, 44, 50, 52 and 54 seem to give the relatives of a murdered individual a choice between imposition of the death penalty and exaction of reimbursement. Indeed, Article 51 gives the guardian of the murdered person the right to perform the execution or else to hire another to carry it out.

Article 97 of the Law of *Hodoud* and *Qesas* also reveals a disregard for the right to seek pardon, commutation, or appeal:

"If fornication is proved by testimony or confession, its punishment must be carried out immediately, except in exceptional cases such as sickness or pregnancy."

Article 14 (5) of the International Covenant on Civil and Political Rights provides that: "Everyone convicted of a crime shall have the right to his conviction and sentence being reviewed by a higher tribunal according to law." Such a guarantee of appeal is particularly important where the charge carries the death penalty, as in certain fornication charges.

Article 6 (5) of the International Covenant on Civil and Political

Rights specifies: "Sentence of death shall not be imposed for crimes committed by persons below eighteen years of age and shall not be carried out on pregnant women." Certain provisions in the Law of *Hodoud* and *Qesas* protect women from execution or punishment that might harm an infant or an unborn child, see, for example, Article 48. Article 23 of the Law of *Hodoud* and *Qesas* suggests that a defendant need not be of full age to be accused of an offence such as murder. There do not appear to be any limitations on the execution of those who have committed offences when under 18.

Article 6 of the International Covenant on Civil and Political Rights also forbids executions which are "contrary to the provisions of the present Covenant", thereby incorporating by reference the procedural guarantees of fairness set forth in Article 14 of the Covenant, which are discussed more fully in the next section of this memorandum. In as much as the Law of *Hodoud* and *Qesas* contains provisions which create risks of procedural unfairness, Article 6 forbids use of the death penalty in such cases.

5. *Fair trial guarantees*

Amnesty International opposes the detention of political prisoners who have not been brought to trial within a reasonable time and any trial procedures relating to such prisoners that do not conform to internationally recognized norms. As indicated above, Amnesty International opposes the death penalty and is, therefore, all the more concerned if a death penalty is imposed pursuant to procedures not consistent with internationally recognized standards of fairness.

Internationally recognized norms for fair procedure in criminal cases are set forth in Articles 7-11 of the Universal Declaration of Human Rights, Articles 6, 14 and 15 of the International Covenant on Civil and Political Rights, and common Article 3 of the four Geneva Conventions of 12 August 1949.

The Islamic Penal Code of Iran does not present a complete picture of the procedures used in determining the penal responsibility of those accused of offences in the Islamic Republic of Iran. Nevertheless, the Penal Code does not provide adequate protection for the rights of the accused and contains a number of provisions which may have encouraged violations of the fair trial rights of those accused of criminal offences in the Islamic Republic of Iran. This is a cause for concern for Amnesty International where charges are of a political nature, and when the penalty for the offence constitutes torture, or other cruel, inhuman or degrading punishment, or when the death penalty is applied.

A. *Problems of proof*

Article 27 of the Law of *Hodoud* and *Qesas* describes the methods "by which a murder is proved in court" as follows: "1. Confession 2. Testimony 3. *Qassameh* [oath] 4. Knowledge of the judge".

The prevalent use of oaths and the testimony of "righteous men" as methods of proof in the Law of *Hodoud* and *Qesas* raises serious questions about the "full equality" of fair procedures required by Article 10 of the Universal Declaration of Human Rights, and about provision of "all the guarantees necessary for [the accused's] defence" required by Article 11 of the Declaration.

Oath-taking or testimony by a "righteous" male has such profound legal implications that the judicial system accepts such oaths or testimony as sufficient proof of either guilt or innocence. For example, Article 33 (a) of the Law of *Hodoud* and *Qesas* states that premeditated "murder is proved by the testimony of two righteous males". Article 33 (b) states that quasi-intentional "murder or culpable homicide is proved by the testimony of two righteous males, or one righteous male and two righteous females, or one righteous male and the oath of the complainant". Another example may be found in Articles 148-151 of the Law of *Hodoud* and *Qesas*:

> Article 148: "Sodomy is proved by the testimony of four
> righteous men who must have observed it."
>
> Article 149: "If fewer than four righteous men testify,
> sodomy is not proved and the witnesses shall be condemned
> to punishment for *qazf* [malicious accusation]."
>
> Article 150: "Testimony of women alone, or together with a
> man, does not prove sodomy."
>
> Article 151: "The *Shari'a* judge may act according to his
> own knowledge which is derived from customary methods."

A charge of being *mohareb* (at enmity with God) or *mofsed fil arz* (corrupt on earth) may be proved according to Article 201 of the Law of *Hodoud* and *Qesas* by means either of a confession or of the testimony of two "righteous men".

Such provisions relating to the proof of criminal charges clearly present serious difficulties as regards the fairness, equality and guarantees of the defence of those accused who have to rely on women witnesses. The use of oaths as proof also violates Article 14 (3)(e) of the International Covenant on Civil and Political Rights in that the accused should have the right to examine prosecution witnesses.

Reliance on "knowledge of the judge" for proof of a criminal charge also presents serious problems of fairness. Articles 10 and 11 of the Universal Declaration of Human Rights contain the most relevant summary of international standards of fairness in criminal proceedings:

> Article 10: "Everyone is entitled in full equality to a fair and public hearing by an independent and impartial tribunal, in the determination of his rights and obligations and of any charge against him."

> Article 11 (1): "Everyone charged with a penal offence has the right to be presumed innocent until proved guilty according to law in a public trial at which he has had all the guarantees necessary for his defence."

If a judge relies solely on his own knowledge about a criminal charge, the question arises as to whether the tribunal was sufficiently "impartial" when deciding on the charge. Similarly, if the judge relies on his own knowledge, the question arises as to whether the person charged will be presumed innocent or will have "all the guarantees necessary for his defence".

Article 120 of the Law of *Hodoud* and *Qesas* evidently recognizes at least some of these difficulties in that it requires a judge "acting in his own knowledge" on a charge of fornication to "mention the grounds on which his knowledge is based". This provision is lacking elsewhere in the Law of *Hodoud* and *Qesas*.

B. *Presumption of Innocence*

The Islamic Penal Code of Iran does not appear to make effective provision for the presumption of innocence. Article 37 of the Constitution of the Islamic Republic of Iran proclaims this basic right, which is enshrined in Article 11 of the Universal Declaration of Human Rights and in Article 14 of the International Covenant on Civil and Political Rights. Nevertheless, this memorandum has already mentioned, in this regard, the use of a judge's own knowledge and the profound effect of the testimony of "righteous men" or the oath of the complainant. Article 38 of the Law of *Hodoud* and *Qesas* states that in "cases of doubt [about a murder charge], first the defendant is asked to furnish valid witnesses". Such provisions suggest that the Penal Code lacks an effective recognition of the presumption of innocence.

6. Recommendations

The following recommendations are respectfully submitted to the authorities of the Islamic Republic of Iran responsible for considering changes in the Islamic Penal Code of Iran which was promulgated on a trial basis for five years in 1982 (1361) and 1983 (1362) and thus should be reconsidered during the next year or two. The following recommendations are based on Amnesty International's reading of the Islamic Penal Code of Iran in the light of the principles of international human rights law relevant to its own statutory concerns.

1.   The Islamic Penal Code of Iran should be amended so as to replace the punishments of stoning to death, crucifixion, mutilation, and flogging with some other punishments not involving torture or cruel, inhuman, or degrading punishment and not resulting in death.

2.   In revising the Islamic Penal Code of Iran and adopting the Penal Procedure Code, provisions should be introduced to prevent torture or cruel, inhuman, or degrading treatment or punishment, in addition to those provisions forbidding torture which have already been adopted in accordance with Article 38 of the Constitution of the Islamic Republic of Iran. The preventive measures, which should be introduced to help ensure that confessions are not made under duress or torture, should include: first, safeguards to ensure that incommunicado detention does not become an opportunity for torture. All prisoners should be brought before a judicial authority promptly after being taken into custody and relatives, lawyers, and doctors should have prompt and regular access to them. Second, prisoners should be promptly told of their rights, including the right to lodge complaints about their treatment. There should be regular independent visits of inspection to places of detention. There should be separation of the authorities responsible for detention from those in charge of interrogation. Third, all complaints and reports of torture should be impartially and thoroughly investigated, the methods and findings of such investigations being made public. Complainants and witnesses should be protected from intimidation. Fourth, there should be adequate procedures for challenging the use of confessions in criminal proceedings, where such confessions or other evidence are obtained through torture.

3.   The Law of *Hodoud* and *Qesas* should be amended so as to reduce reliance on confessions as the primary method of proof and to diminish the incentive for law enforcement officials to inflict torture or impose other forms of duress in order to obtain such confessions. Prosecutors should be encouraged to rely less on confessions and more on testimony by witnesses or other forms of evidence.

4.   The Islamic Penal Code of Iran should be amended so as to define very clearly what constitute offences against the government or internal security, and to ensure that only those who engage in

violence against the state or advocate such violence shall be punished.

5.   The Islamic Penal Code of Iran should be amended in order to provide safeguards against the incarceration of prisoners of conscience. Existing laws should be revised to ensure that no one who has not used or advocated violence is imprisoned for political, religious or other conscientiously held beliefs or because of ethnic origin, sex, colour or language.

6.   The Law of *Hodoud* and *Qesas* should be amended so as to abolish the death penalty and replace it with other punishments not involving torture or cruel, inhuman, or degrading punishment.

7.   The Islamic Penal Code of Iran should be amended so as to provide for pardon, commutation of sentence and appeal, as specified in Articles 6 and 14 of the International Covenant on Civil and Political Rights. The Law of *Hodoud* and *Qesas* should be amended so as to remove any provisions which require the immediate imposition of punishment thus infringing the right to pardon, commutation of sentence and appeal.

8.   In revising the Islamic Penal Code of Iran and adopting the Penal Procedure Code, provisions should be introduced to provide the procedural safeguards contained in Articles 7 to 11 of the Universal Declaration of Human Rights and Articles 6, 14 and 15 of the International Covenant on Civil and Political Rights. Among these procedural protections are the right to freedom from arbitrary arrest, the right to notice of charges, the right to a prompt and public trial before an impartial and independent tribunal, the right to the presumption of innocence, the right to legal assistance of one's choice, the right to all the guarantees necessary for the defence, including the right to have defence witnesses, and the right to examine prosecution witnesses.

9.   The Law of *Hodoud* and *Qesas* should be amended so as to provide that no one should be required to serve a sentence or suffer a penalty greater than the law provided at the time the offence was committed, in accordance with Article 15 of the International Covenant on Civil and Political Rights.

10.   The Law of *Hodoud* and *Qesas* should be amended so as to allow evidence by one witness to be evaluated according to the same principles as that of any other witness.

Testimonies

The following testimonies describe the treatment received by four former prisoners of conscience and political prisoners. Although Amnesty International cannot vouch for every detail in these accounts, it believes they illustrate the kinds of human rights violations being carried out in Iran, as they are representative of many such testimonies collected by the organization.

Details such as names and dates which could identify the four have been omitted or amended because of their fear of reprisals against relatives in Iran.

Testimony

The following testimony was given by a woman who was taken from her home in November 1983 by Revolutionary Guards after they had failed to arrest her husband. She spent 14 months in Evin and Gohar Dasht prisons until she was released one week after a five-minute court appearance. Although not tortured herself, she describes seeing and speaking to many who were.

I was born in Kermanshah [now called Bakhtaran] and went to primary and secondary school there. In 1977 I then went to the Esfahan College of Technology. I was suspended for three terms because I joined in an anti-Shah demonstration.

After the revolution I began to be involved in political activities until I was arrested in November 1983. My husband belonged to the same organization. When the Revolutionary Guards came to my home it was in order to arrest my husband who was out of the house. They had no warrant for my arrest, but when they could not find him they said they would hold me for just two hours to ask me a few questions. I was in prison for 14 months.

I was blindfolded and taken to Evin prison and was taken along a corridor to the main offices. On one side of Block 209 there were interrogation rooms and on the other side people were held. There is a staircase leading to the basement which is used for torture.

Another part of the upstairs corridor is used as a dispensary and surgery. Prisoners are usually taken there immediately after torture. All along the corridor people were squashed into rows or kneeling down; all of them were blindfolded. I was wearing a *chador* and could lift the blindfold very slightly and see beneath it. I could see men were sitting there with very swollen feet and legs. You could see bloodstains in the corridor which were deliberately not cleaned up in order to frighten the prisoners. There were prisoners along the corridor too, held suspended by their wrists, which were tied together, from a bar on top of the door. People were so positioned that only the tips of their toes were touching the floor and sometimes they would be left hanging there for days on end. Both men and women were treated like this. There was a prisoner suspended in each doorway. One of them had been arrested in connection with Kurdish political activities and I discovered he had been there for a very long time. There were also places used for suspension in the basement. In the corridors some people were tied to radiators, others were allowed to squat. There wasn't enough room to sit comfortably. If people wanted to go to the lavatory, they had to move about so as to attract attention. People who had been tortured couldn't stand up anyway. Many people's feet and legs were infected.

When I was arrested, I told the guards my husband was out and that he would soon return. So they stayed in the house for four days before they took me away. They changed the guards, who stayed outside in the corridors of the block of flats while the family stayed upstairs. The apartment was on the fourth floor and the guards stayed in the corridor for four days, not attracting any attention, trying not to let our neighbours know they were there because they didn't want my husband to be frightened away. My son, then 18 months old, was very frightened and wouldn't stop crying. This made the guards very nervous and they kept asking me to get the child to shut up. The guards certainly didn't want our neighbours to know what was happening in case they alerted my husband. Eventually, they realized he wasn't going to return.

When they finally removed me to Evin, the guards realized my husband wasn't going to come back. Fortunately, they seemed to know nothing about my own political activities, but they did realize that I probably didn't know where my husband was.

On the stairs in Block 209 at Evin prison, people were lying covered by blankets. They left me there for some time so that I could hear the shouts and moans of other people being beaten. I stayed in the corridor blindfold for eight days. In the morning they took me down to the basement and in the evening they brought me back. I was only allowed to go to the lavatory once a day and was constantly cursed and sworn at. I wasn't beaten and I wasn't physically tortured. I was interrogated and only once asked to tell all. This was on my fourth day at Evin. I said I knew nothing and could tell them absolutely nothing. When I asked to telephone home to find out if my son was all right they told me he was in Evin too but later I found this was untrue.

Downstairs, the chamber was huge, one large room. They took me through it once a day on the way to the toilets of which there are about three or four. I could see people lying under their blankets and cables were lying around too. At the end of the eight days I was taken to a cell in Section 3 Block 209, which I shared with two other people. The cell was meant for just one person but contained three. It was approximately $2\frac{1}{2}$ by $1\frac{1}{2}$ metres and contained a small toilet and washbasin. It was in a very modern section. Because there was a toilet in the cell, we weren't let out of it at all except for interrogation. One of the other two people, who was 22, was pregnant. The other, also aged 22, belonged to a student organization. The pregnant woman had been arrested in Tehran with her husband on suspicion when she was waiting to leave town at a bus station. Her husband had been badly tortured and thrown down in front of her. She too was tortured. Her hair was pulled and she was sworn at and taken downstairs to hear the shouting of other people being tortured. When her husband was brought to her he had an intravenous drip attached. At one stage, she was taken to wait outside the interrogation room while he was being tortured. She heard a terrible shout. Afterwards when she saw him she asked him why he had shouted so terribly. He said he couldn't explain but something very bad had happened — the word he used is normally used about sexual abuse.

This cell-mate also told me about a girl who had been beaten very hard on the feet with a cable. The soles of her feet were very badly injured. They wanted to get addresses out of her. She refused to give any information and was tied to one of the radiators. When a guard passed he touched her and she was sure he was going to rape her. In fact, she was not raped but suffered greatly as a result of psychological pressure and bled badly from the beatings three times. She was in solitary confinement for 40 days before being joined by two people. The pregnant woman was told that she would not be tortured because she was pregnant but that they would start as soon as she had given birth. I knew about other cases of pregnant women being tortured.

One day they made us run to the main gates of the prison and didn't tell us why. They took us to the guard room by the gate and waited for a car. There were five women in this room; one was from the *Mojahedine*, two belonged to other groups, and there was a writer and myself. We were actually allowed to talk to each other for a while. A mother complained that her children were in a very bad psychological state. She thought they were being drugged and given tranquillizers to keep them quiet. When we were in the minibus, we realized we were being taken to Gohar Dasht prison. The *Mojahed* girl told us she was told this during her interrogation and warned that if she didn't supply information she would be sent there as a punishment. The transfer took place in December 1983. Gohar Dasht is apparently notorious for torture, harsh treatment and as a punishment centre. On the way, the guards joked and called us Gohar Dasht inmates. It was an ordinary minibus so we weren't blindfolded. When we arrived, they blindfolded us with very long blindfolds, bound tightly. They were rather different from the sorts of blindfold worn at Evin where you can sometimes see out from underneath. We were each taken to a solitary confinement cell and separated. I never saw the children and their mother again.

I spent four and a half months in solitary confinement. Throughout I was never interrogated. It was a form of punishment — just to leave you there in a state of suspense. Every time I saw a guard I asked how long I was going to stay there and he would say, "that depends on you — if you write a note saying you want to talk, that will be fine".

The cells were just like at Evin. I left my cell only once a week for 20 minutes to take a shower. That was the only time I was allowed out. Sometimes I could hear that the children were still there — I could occasionally hear them crying. They were evidently in a cell like mine. Whenever they cried the guards would shout at the women to keep them quiet. After about 22 or 23 days, I didn't hear the children any more. Later I heard that they had been taken back home but that their mothers had stayed on. The children were shut in the cell for 15 days. After 15 days, the young boy was let out and ran around like a greyhound just escaped from a cage. He dashed madly about and ran all over the place, kicking all the doors and darting here, there, and everywhere; the guards couldn't keep up with him. Finally, they got hold of him and put him back. Of course, I never saw any of this. I couldn't see out of my cell but I could hear it going on — and after a while in solitary confinement you begin seeing things with your ears. Gohar Dasht is a dreadful, dangerous place — it's so frightening. Almost everyone is in solitary confinement and every morning they beat up most of the prisoners, men and women. I was never beaten, but I was certainly sworn at regularly. And I heard moaning every day. The main guard or one of the people under him used to lash people with cables and whips. The guards also hit people with shoes and slippers.

When we were in Evin you couldn't hear torture from the cells in Block 209 but in Gohar Dasht never a moment passed without your hearing the shouts of people being tortured. You could feel it taking place; you could feel the person in the next cell being dragged out. The beating had nothing to do with interrogation — that's why Gohar Dasht is so frightening. It's just part of prison life. It's not done simply to extract information. If, for instance, they entered a cell and saw a mark or a line on the wall, even if it was there before, they would say, "Why is that there? What did you do it for? You're fined 200 *tomans*"; then they'd beat you.

Gohar Dasht is meant both for prisoners who have been tried and for untried detainees. But usually you go there after having been through Evin. Then they take you back to Evin for interrogation. There's practically no interrogation in Gohar Dasht. And there are places there called black holes — small cells the size of a table which are specially used for punishment. They contain no toilets or wash-basins.

After four and a half months, I was taken back to Evin where I shared a cell with a 22-year-old girl, a supporter of the Organization of *Fedayan* guerrillas. She had spent seven months in Gohar Dasht and she had been sentenced to 15 years' imprisonment. She had also been in Qezel-Hesar prison. She was sent from Evin to Qezel-Hesar, then to Gohar Dasht, then to Evin. She arrived back at Evin when I was there. In Iran, a prisoner does not go through the usual cycle of interrogation, trial, sentence, etc. In Iran, the interrogation goes on regardless of what stage has been reached in the judicial proceedings — whether it's after the trial, at night, or at any time — no matter what your sentence, interrogation goes on.

I was in solitary confinement for four and a half months — the minimum being four months and the average about a year. Sometimes you get punished because you communicate by banging your plate or spoon or something just to make contact with other prisoners. You're not allowed any contact with other prisoners. Even when you go for a shower it's in a cell — there's nobody else around.

There are so many cases of people, prisoners, being mentally disturbed, that it's hard not to get like that yourself. When I was in Section 1 of the women's block, I met a woman there. She had been arrested in 1980 when she was a schoolgirl. She was moved after a month to Evin. In about June 1980 she was taken to court and had a brief trial. She was sentenced to 15 years' imprisonment. When I saw her she couldn't talk about her trial. After she was sentenced, they realized that she was still very loyal to her political organization (the

Mojahedine) and took her to Gohar Dasht, where she stayed for nearly a year. From Gohar Dasht she was taken to Section 2 of the women's block at Evin and stayed there for some time. Eventually, they realized she was too ill to stay there and they took her to the sanatorium at Evin, which is a new block, very similar to Gohar Dasht. There are separate cells there. From there she returned to Section 1 where I saw her. When I saw her face I thought she was at least 30. In fact, she was 19 at the time. The only thing about her which made me think that perhaps she was under 30 was the teenage spots she still had on her face. Her first question to me was what year and what month was it. There were now six of us in a 4 by $4\frac{1}{2}$ metres cell. I realized that her face and her eyes weren't normal, but fortunately one of us was a doctor who realized she was mentally disturbed. The girl would just sit and smile all the time, then suddenly start laughing hysterically, then burst into tears. Afterwards, she would lie down, pull a blanket over her and sleep. She never wanted to eat but every couple of days or so she'd eat just one or two bits. This pattern persisted.

Three times a day we were allowed out to the lavatory, and one day, when the guard opened the door, she ran out shouting the name of one of her friends. We followed her and tried to catch up with her. She was in the hall banging her head violently against the wall. We couldn't control her. Finally a guard came, put his hand over her mouth and dragged her upstairs. She returned to the cell two hours later having quietened down. After another two hours' calm she began the cycle all over again. Her behaviour was so unsettling that we were practically turning into lunatics ourselves. All of us were nervous. She laughed very loudly, and when she did the doctor would cry quietly in a corner. Finally, the doctor asked to speak to the person responsible for the women's block and told her that she needed to be taken away for treatment and that she should be moved in order to get psychological treatment. The guard said repeatedly: "No, she's not like that really. She's pretending, but if she does need treatment, we'll send her back to the sanatorium." This is their policy: they put people in solitary confinement, then return them to the cell block and then put them in solitary. They treat them as though they were normal and consider their strange behaviour a sign of resistance.

We spent about 18 days with her and several days later the same thing happened again when she ran out into the corridor. This time they took her away for good, probably to the sanatorium.

Another mentally unbalanced woman was a distant relative. She was arrested once before in 1981 in Esfahan. Then she had tried to commit suicide by setting herself on fire with a kerosene lamp. When

I saw her in Evin prison her skin was badly scarred with burns. They wanted to execute her in Esfahan but they apparently decided not to when they realized that she was so unbalanced. So they finally released her, but she was rearrested somewhere else. This was in early 1984. They tied her hands together to prevent her from hurting herself. She was taken to Evin prison around August or September 1984.

When I saw her she was in the corridor with her hands tied to the radiator in Section 1 of the women's block. Her feet were badly swollen from being beaten. I actually didn't recognize her, but she recognized me and called out to me. As I frequently passed by her when I was being taken to the lavatory, we sometimes exchanged a few words. When she saw me her face would light up and she would call me aunty — I don't know why. You could see her joy when she saw me. She was tied to the radiator for about two weeks and finally they took her to the courtyard, but when she was taken out there she was tied from behind to the window. She was incontinent and had soiled herself badly — the smell of excrement in the corridor was awful. She behaved just like a two- or three-year-old when taken to the lavatory — she simply soiled herself and her clothes.

She was very wet and dirty. And she ate like a small child or a retarded person — her food spilled down her as she ate with her hand. She was removed then and I don't know what happened to her after that. After my release, I heard that her mother, sister and brother were all in prison — although I believe her mother was released after three years. Her sister is still in prison, her brother too, although there are rumours that he may have been executed. All of them were supporters of the *Mojahedine*.

If people are not tortured physically they are punished by being put in different cells or different prisons — it's all meant to unsettle you. I was taken to a new block which was the sanatorium and I saw a girl there who was exceedingly ill — really very mentally unbalanced — so much so that she ate her own excrement. I never saw this happen but I could hear the arguments going on between the girl and a guard who was telling her off about it. And there was a mother in the sanatorium who was so nervous that she constantly beat her child. You see, there is a general atmosphere of fear and uncertainty; everyone suffers from this, everyone has psychological problems, no one can be normal there.

Out of the 14 months I spent in prison I was in solitary confinement for nine months, either in solitary confinement in the strictest sense, or in cells intended for one person but where there were two or three of us. But for the nine months there was no contact whatsoever with the outside world, no reading material, nothing. In that period I tried to look after myself and take hold of myself because I could feel myself under pressure and becoming psychologically unbalanced at times. No one had questioned or interrogated me, I was still waiting for someone to question me, and this brought with it a lot of anxiety too. All the time I saw strange things, like pictures in my mind, and I felt that everybody was an informer. I imagined I saw my husband and that he was an interrogator and even, can you imagine, I thought my tiny son was one, too.

The first visit I had lasted for five minutes. It was my father who visited me at Gohar Dasht prison after six months.

Until my period in solitary confinement I trusted everybody — all the prisoners — but during the final days of my imprisonment I became much more cautious. When I went to the new block I realized that I had become somewhat mentally unbalanced and when I first got back from Gohar Dasht, when I laughed the others told me that I sounded hysterical and I realized they were right. For three days I couldn't eat or sleep. I wanted to find out which of the prisoners were good people and which informers. One of the "repentant" prisoners, who was next to me, kept telling me not to trust anyone except her. I suffered from this lack of trust — the unsettling feeling of not being able to trust anybody — and at the same time a sense of beginning to be under religious pressure. Suddenly one day a loudspeaker started broadcasting prayers and religious speeches. This troubled me greatly. I kept asking the guards why they were broadcasting these prayers and told a guard crossly to turn it down as no one was listening. It genuinely bothered me.

The pressure at Gohar Dasht prison was so heavy that when I was sent back to Evin I almost felt as though they were releasing me — it was, in a way, like going home to get back to Block 209. I thought I was being taken there for interrogation, but it still didn't happen — they just asked me a few questions about my husband and how was I arrested, and who were my husband's friends, and I just said I didn't know. After a week I shared a cell with a woman of 36 whose husband was executed under the Shah.

A week later the cell door opened and they chucked in another woman as if she were a corpse. She was 24. Her feet were very badly swollen and we could see the marks of an operation on her feet with strange new growths of flesh. She had tried to commit suicide by cutting her veins in both forearms, which were now very heavily bandaged. She had been arrested with her husband on the road to Kurdistan. She had been tortured in Tabriz then taken to Section 3000 (the old joint *Komiteh*) run by Revolutionary Guards. She was taken to one room in Section 3000 and her husband to another, and they were beaten up. She lay on her stomach with her hands tied to the bed for two days and nights and they whipped her at intervals while she was tied to the wooden bed. Then her hands were tied diagonally behind her back with weighted handcuffs, one hand over the shoulder, the other beneath. The more you move the tighter it becomes and it pulls dreadfully on the shoulder. Afterwards, she was kept for three months in a corridor at *Komiteh* premises. Her husband was kept there for 10 months under the same conditions in the same place. Once a week the blindfold was removed and they were taken for a shower. Twice, while out in the corridor she had tried to commit suicide, once with electricity and once by taking a lot of pills, probably antibiotics that she had been saving up — she'd asked for them because she had diarrhoea. When she had got hold of the electric wires the guards had come and held her. She stayed in Section 3000 for 16 months without having any visitors or getting anything from outside. After the 16 months were up she and her husband were moved to Evin. There she was treated as though she had just been arrested — taken to the basement and for about a week beaten every other day. She was suspended by her wrists for four days and nights. She was exhausted but couldn't sleep. After four days she said "Please let me down, I'll tell you everything". Then she said, "If you just let me sleep for an hour I'll talk." Then they put her in the large hall with a blanket for the night. She had hidden a small safety pin in her *chador* and that was when she tried to open her veins and cut her wrists. She bled for a while, then tried to cut other veins. In fact, she tried to do this in several places. After an hour she fainted and a guard found her. The guard summoned the interrogators. They photographed her, then took her to surgery where she was treated. Afterwards, she was kept blindfold in the corridor for another month. They interrogated her and told her that she would be executed unless she repented. She told them that they, not she, were the counter-revolutionaries. Then they put her in our cell. It was such a disturbing sight to see her — and not only see her, for she smelt dreadfully of stale blood. She hadn't been allowed to wash or bathe and she was in very poor health. She had blood in her urine and a vaginal infection. It was at this time that she joined us. Then she was sent to the sanatorium.

Twenty days before I was released I was taken to a building called the court where there was a mullah behind a desk who must have been in his early twenties. There were four chairs on one side of the room and I sat down with three other women. None of us had anything in common politically; each of us had been arrested for different reasons. We gave our names one by one and were each asked which organization we had been arrested in connection with and what our political activities were. I said that I had been arrested because they couldn't find my husband, and another woman said she had been at a party and had no political affiliations at all. The court convened for no more than five minutes. There was no one else in the room, but there were interruptions the whole time. The judge was asked if he was free to do this or that, or when he could talk to this person or that — it was all very strange. After five minutes we were told to leave the room and there were no further questions. A week later I was released. I think the others were too. A relative guaranteed me. He's not allowed to leave the country for two years now. He had to undertake to produce me if I am required. I was never informed that I'd been acquitted. I was told one day to go for interrogation and when I was there saw my father and realized I was being released. I had to sign a paper promising not to participate in political activities in future.

Testimony

A student and teacher at Tehran University, this woman was arrested because of her political activities, but never charged or tried. She was detained from September 1981 to March 1982 at Evin and Qezel-Hesar prisons and was tortured during her detention. According to her, hundreds of people were killed while she was in prison.

I was born in 1955. I was a student at Tehran University and a teacher. I was imprisoned from September 1981 to March 1982 in Evin and later in Qezel-Hesar. I was arrested at 9pm one day when two armed Revolutionary Guards came with an arrest warrant to take me from my home. I lived in Tehran. My son, aged three and a half, was with me. I asked what I should do about the child. I was told to leave him there even though I insisted I should take him with me. They told me that I would be back in two or three days' time.

I went with them in a Fiat car. I had to blindfold myself with a headscarf and sit on the floor of the car. We reached Evin prison at about 10pm. The house had been searched earlier when my husband was arrested. Nothing had been found.

At Evin I had to sit on the lawn. They put a big heavy sack over my head which came well down over my chest so I found it difficult to breathe. There was a lot of noise. I could hear a guard shouting "why don't they send an order for his execution?" I didn't know who they were talking about. They told me that the interrogator was not there so I would have to stay overnight and at 10.30am next day the interrogator would arrive.

I was taken to a cell the size of a small blanket. There was only the floor to lie on and the light was soon switched off. There was no lavatory or sink and nobody else in the cell. I was soon in complete darkness. I could hear a boy being beaten hard on the other side of the door and I heard them telling him that he was going to be executed. He cried and called for his mother. I stayed there until morning when it was still dark. They told the boy to get up as he was going to be executed. I could hear him moaning and I tried to make sympathetic noises to attract his attention and comfort him but he didn't pay any attention.

Several hours later I saw light under my door. I banged on it and asked to be let out to go to the lavatory. A young boy came and asked who had brought me here. He told me to blindfold myself and follow him and he took me there and back. Half an hour later I was blindfolded again and taken away. There were other prisoners around and they told me to hang on to a man's coat-tail and follow him. I went into a large hallway where there were many people and a woman guard came and hit me on the chest and told me to speak and confess or else I would see incredible things. There was a lot of crying and wailing; then I was told: "we are going to take off your blindfold. You mustn't look to the side, just look straight ahead." I opened my eyes and saw a young boy hanging from a tree. Both his arms were bandaged up to the elbows and both legs up to the knees. He was very thin and his name was written on a card round his neck. A guard stood next to the boy and poked the body with a stick making it turn around and around. Meanwhile other guards watched the prisoners to see their reactions. Then we were blindfolded again and taken for interrogation.

I noted that a lot of women had been arrested on the streets for not dressing correctly. They had been given white sheets to cover themselves with and were lying on the floor. There were so many of them that even their breathing was noisy. They had to squeeze up on the floor and some guards came and asked if anyone had not seen the corpse. I said I had already seen it and was told I had to see it again, so they took me back. Somebody told me that I should take pity on my own youthfulness and confess all I knew and had heard. In the yard I could hear slogans being shouted. I hadn't had any breakfast and I just sat in the room. I was squatting there when I heard my name being called. I raised my hand and was taken into another room and made to sit on a chair facing the corner. I was asked my name and if I had any appointments with political colleagues in the next few days. I said no. There were three other people in the room being tortured and interrogated. I was wearing a *chador* and tried to look around it at one of the people lying on the floor near me. His hands were tied behind his back and he was lying on his stomach on the floor and shouting out. He was being beaten with a thick cable all over his body. All he could say was "water".

My interrogator asked who I had seen yesterday and who I was due to see that day, and I said I had only gone to the park with my young son. Then I realized that the room was entirely silent and that the man next to me had become silent. My interrogator said: "Within a few hours we will get everything out of you." When I refused to confess I was blindfolded and told to lie down on the floor. One of them whipped my feet with a heavy cable. I was wearing socks but the first lash was so painful that I jumped up and ran around the room. Then they tied my hands behind my back, and my feet together, removing my socks. They covered my head with a blanket and beat me again on my back and feet, telling me to confess which political organization I belonged to and to give the names of my political comrades.

I don't know how long it continued. At one point I pretended to be unconscious, but they just beat me harder, accusing me of trying to fool them. When they finally stopped, my feet were bleeding badly, especially around the toe-nails.

They said they were going to lunch and left me sitting on a chair but I was shaking so much I couldn't sit on it. When I went to the lavatory there was blood in my urine. I asked if I could lie on the floor since I was in such pain but they wouldn't let me.

They brought me some food but I couldn't eat it. Then they interrogated me again and brought lots of white paper for me to write on. I heard another prisoner, near me, saying that he had told everything he knew and there was no need to hit him any more. They said, "Nothing doing. Some people can write more quickly after they have been beaten." I could hear cries all the time — shouting and moans. All the noises I heard women, young girls and boys make are beyond description. I was asked where I was on the day Beheshti was killed... They were angry because I wouldn't answer their questions and shoved me hard against the wall. My head struck the wall and I felt dizzy. My eyes watered for some time. After my release, I went to a specialist for a brain scan and was told I had a blood clot caused by torture. However, it will probably disappear after a time.

I couldn't write as my hands were shaking so much and I badly needed water. I was told to sit and write. I was blindfold but when I needed to write I could lift the blindfold up a bit.

At 5pm, I was taken to the corridor. While I was sitting in the corridor near the interrogation section a guard came again and asked who hadn't yet seen the corpse and who wanted to see it again. Some of us actually raised our hands and I was asked why I didn't want to see it again. I replied that I had seen it twice. Those who raised their hands actually were taken to see the corpse again. I was left where I was, then later taken to another room where I was with about 20 others. Each of us had to put her hand on the shoulder of the person in front and we marched in line out through the courtyard. My feet were very swollen and I couldn't wear my shoes. We walked over pebbles and it was exceedingly painful. The guard forced us to walk over empty flower beds which was very painful. The guard led the first prisoner by holding on to one end of a hosepipe, the woman holding the other end. He had another length of hosepipe he used as a whip when some of us couldn't walk fast enough. We were taken to a special room. There was a brick entrance hall and we stood there, still blindfold. They asked us all questions: our names, surnames and why we had been arrested. I was told that since I was not one of the faithful I should not be wearing a *chador* — that I had no right to wear one. All the guards here were women, and I was told to go to cell block No. 1 where I was given a plastic tray, a plastic cup and a spoon. I was allowed to remove my blindfold and I could then see the hall was very small with two desks with guards sitting behind them, vats [of food] and in the corner leaning against a wall many lengths of hosepipe to serve as whips, and straps to be used as blindfolds. There was a door leading into a courtyard made of exceedingly thick glass through which the light could barely penetrate. We were told by a guard that we were being taken to a cell which had been equipped by SAVAK and was no ordinary cell because it was full of hidden cameras and microphones.

Block No. 1 consisted of a big room and two small rooms full of people. The first person I saw was a three-year-old boy. I grabbed him thinking that he was my son and asked him why he was there. Then his mother appeared and said he was her co-accused as they had both been arrested at the same time at a demonstration. Ninety-nine per cent of those in the cell had been tortured. There were about 120 of us and the whole place was only 65 or 66 square metres. Each of us asked how the others had been arrested and treated. My feet were very painful and bleeding and my cell-mates calmed me down and I fell asleep believing that I would be tortured again the next day. At 5am an angry guard arrived and clapped his hands. We all woke up very frightened. Yelling "Militia!" he told us sarcastically to get up and keep our appointments and distribute our pamphlets. Everyone's face turned pale and everyone was trembling, shaking and nervous. Many people were from the *Mojahedine* and other left-wing organizations, and next day 20 more joined us. At night the names of people due for execution were called out and they were executed before dawn. The guard came and opened the door and summoned those who were to be executed. There were seven sections in this place. Ours was on the first floor, and on each floor were similar women's cells, and people to be executed were brought here from all the other floors down to the first floor. In the end, there was a huge crowd waiting to be executed. About 20 new people came to our cell. They had been made to lie in graves for two or three hours while being questioned. Their average age was 17. Most of them were young — either students or school children — and some had no idea why they were there.

One night a young girl called Tahereh was brought straight from the courtroom to our cell. She had just been sentenced to death, and was confused and agitated. She didn't seem to know why she was there. She settled down to sleep next to me, but at intervals she woke up with a start, terrified, and grasped me, asking if it were true that she really would be executed. I put my arms around her and tried to comfort her, and reassure her that it wouldn't happen, but at about 4am they came for her and she was taken away to be executed. She was 16 years old.

No visitors were allowed. There were next to no toilets and we were not allowed toothbrushes even though some of us had badly swollen gums. We had no change of underwear — and there were now 180 of us in the cell with new people coming in all the time. Nobody cared whether there was room for more or not before fresh people were brought in, and all of us were tortured. There were three old women, one of whom had helped her sons to escape via the roof of her home. She had been beaten so much on the breasts that they were extremely swollen. She was over 60 and she had been cursed for giving milk to her children. They had shown her photograph on television and asked anybody who knew her to come forward with information (this was common practice). When she arrived in the cell she was trembling. She was chucked into the cell like a piece of meat and told she should be in hell. The whole cell cried in sympathy as she was so old and she said she had no idea what she had done. Her only sin in life was to be poor.

Eventually there were over 250 people in the cell with only one lavatory and enough food only for 120. Our stomachs were perpetually rumbling with hunger. We couldn't get hold of any scissors to cut our hair. There was only one shower for everybody and eight people had to stand under the same shower for three minutes. Once a week we were given a pair of nail clippers. Those with long hair had a particularly difficult time washing it. I considered myself lucky because when I was arrested I was wearing a blouse and a kind of overall so I could change into one while washing the other. One girl who had been there for three months asked to borrow the blouse so that she could wash her own clothes. She had just soaked her blouse, when she was taken away to be executed. She was 15. The soaked blouse remained for about a week before anybody would touch it. Azadeh, aged 17 and Farideh, aged 16, joined the cell. They were brought in from the court after interrogation. They had been told that they were either to go on television and recant or else be executed. They had refused to be interviewed on television. They arrived at noon, and at 3pm they were taken away; they were executed before the following morning.

Every day the guards brought in a newspaper to show us which of us had been executed. There was a woman of over 60. She had a huge bloated body. She had been taken hostage for her children who were politically active. We were told to pay no attention to her as she was a heretic.

All of us had skin diseases and infections — every one of us. None of us menstruated.

Some of our bodies were very ugly and bloated. We had one bar of soap for every six people and we economized so as to be able to wash, bathe and wash our clothes with it. Once the guards found we had actually been hoarding soap and had hidden three pieces. Twelve of us, including me, were taken away and beaten as a punishment.

I spent three months in Evin. Every day there were fresh stories: personalities destroyed and crushed, but the morale of many remained high. Some people were forced to whip their political comrades, but in fact few agreed to do this.

I was taken for interrogation again. In fact, I was interrogated five times altogether — not every day but after a week, then after three days, then five days later, and so on. Once I saw an old man who looked like a peasant. He was a broom-seller and still had his brooms with him. He was crying. We could hear a guard in the corridor saying "Let's go and beat up that old man" — and they went off and did so. Every night there were executions and I knew most of the victims.

Once — this was in Evin — a woman of 21 arrived who was positively reeking with infection. Her face and mouth were covered with pimples and spots and sores and she stank. Nobody could breathe in her presence, she was so infectious. Some people tried to cover their noses and mouths with cloth when she was near. The woman had suffered so much under torture that she could only urinate standing, and her urine was full of blood and she was quite unable to eat. The other prisoners in the cell asked for her to be taken to surgery for treatment but the guards just closed the door and refused to listen. Three days later they threw her into the corridor and said there was no room in the surgery. She stayed for two days, then was taken away. After about two months somebody saw her in the toilet of the interrogation section: she had been operated on but nobody knew her actual condition.

I was never really tried, but my interrogators had told me I would be kept there until I had told them everything. I believe many people were executed who had done far less serious things than I and that hundreds were killed while I was there.

Testimony

This man was arrested in 1981 and accused of having helped a family leave Iran. During his imprisonment in Evin and Qezel-Hesar prisons, he appeared in court three times and was accused of belonging to various political organizations. After his second appearance he was found not guilty but was not released, he was told, because "young people could smell that I was a counter-revolutionary". He was finally released in March 1984.

I was arrested in July 1981. I was accused of having helped a family to escape from Iran. There was no concrete evidence to prove this. I was simply arrested because I was a close friend of the family. It started the previous night about midnight. Armed Revolutionary Guards came to the house and searched it. They said they were looking for me — this was in Tehran. They stayed until about 5am asking questions and threatening to kill me. They didn't find anything and finally they apologized, but two of them remained in the street outside and watched the house.

I seized the opportunity when they were not looking to go and inform my family who had been away and warn them not to return to the house. At about 10 o'clock in the evening I went back home. I didn't try to escape because many of my friends and relations were politically active and I knew if I wasn't around they would arrest them and ask them about their own activities as well as where I was.

They came to arrest me at midnight. This time they were more violent. They accused me of having guns and political documents. They took my family photographs and slides and documents to do with my work. They struck me with their hands, feet and rifle butts. About 4 or 5am they blindfolded me and took me away. They told me that they were going to take me out of the city and kill me. On the first night I had asked who they were. They said they were *Hizbollah* and didn't need to produce any authorization. On the second night I again asked to see their papers. Instead they showed me a gun and told me it was a *Hizbollahi's* gun and nobody else could have one. Later I gathered that they were actually from Evin, from the Revolutionary Prosecutor's office.

They took me to a place but I didn't know where and put me in a cell measuring $1\frac{1}{2}$ by 2 metres. It was dark. They told me I had 24 hours in which to make up my mind — either to tell them the truth or to be killed. After 24 hours I was taken out of my cell and again blindfolded. I was taken to Evin prison. I knew it was Evin because as the vehicle I was in went through the gates I heard women shouting "Evin prison, Evin prison". As a rule, prisoners' families are outside the prison gates and when they see a blindfolded prisoner being brought in they shout to enable the prisoner to be less disorientated.

When I first arrived at Evin I was put in the corridor. When I thought there were no guards around, I peeped under my blindfold and saw the family I had been questioned about in the corridor. They were all there for the same reason. The mother, sister, husband and sister's husband were there and two of their children, one aged nine, the other 14. There were 11 people in all. They all started talking to each other and clearly were there for the same reason.

Two or three days later I was taken for a preliminary interrogation and for two or three days it was all to do with this family. They wanted to know where the wife and her two sons were. Neither I nor the other detainees knew where they were so the interrogation achieved nothing.

The building where prisoners are kept is separate from the interrogation block. Between interrogations, I was kept in a big room with up to 80 other prisoners. These rooms are known as closed door rooms and the prisoners in them are allowed out three times a day, each time for 10 minutes. I was taken out for interrogation blindfold and taken to the administration building. Interrogations are conducted by workers in the Revolutionary Prosecutor's office.

In 1981 there was a staff shortage so the Revolutionary Guards helped out over interrogation but now (in 1986) the Revolutionary Prosecutor's office does it all. The Revolutionary Guards have their own places too to which they take those they arrest and only at the time of trial would the Revolutionary Prosecutor's office be brought in to deal with such people. They would then be contacted so that a mullah could be sent to pass judgment.

After my interrogation in October I was taken to the interrogation room and told they had information about my activities. They told me to confess or else they would beat me to death.

In the second stage of my interrogation I was accused of being a coordinator of the armed rebellion in Kurdistan, a member of the *Peykar* organization, head of a section of the People's *Mojahedine*, military leader of the People's *Fedai* Organization and the theoretician of the *Tudeh* party.

Interrogation sessions usually started with one of the above. When I denied something they would start torturing me. When I was being tortured I lay on my stomach with my hands fastened to a bed. A man would sit on my neck and squeeze a handkerchief into my mouth. He squeezed hard so it was difficult to breathe. And I had my ankles strapped so that my feet were in the right position to be whipped. Then they would whip my feet, usually 50 to 100 strokes. I was blindfold from time to time. I could see electric cables plaited together. They would remove the plastic covering from the cables so as to leave the wires exposed which made a sharp ball that cut the skin of my feet, stripping the skin. They would stop doing this if a prisoner passed out or if the person who was doing the whipping got tired. Sometimes the claw or ball at the end of the cable would break the bones in the feet.

Another torture was hanging you from a hook in the wall with your toes just touching the ground. At first you would stand on tip-toe but then your legs would start to hurt and you would try to rest your weight on your arms so then your arms hurt. After that you would rest your weight back on your toes but they would still hurt. After a few hours your whole body would be painful. I was tortured like this more than 10 times. Someone else was suspended upside down by the feet and whipped on the back and face. He died under this torture. This was in connection with the same case.

There were other less systematically used tortures like beatings, sticking needles into different parts of the body and blows on the head with wooden sticks. After a time your feet get too injured from being whipped for this form of treatment to be possible or effective any longer. So you get whipped on the back too so that your kidneys start bleeding. Many people had blood in their urine. There was usually no medical treatment after torture — you would just be taken to your cell and left there. Other detainees might help you out. They might know something about first aid, and some people secretly kept pills for emergencies. In acute cases like broken limbs you would be taken to hospital.

My second period of interrogation lasted for between 12 and 15 days. It started with my being accused of being coordinator of military activities in Kurdistan and it proceeded according to schedule. This was the normal way in which they set about interrogating people when they didn't have any information about them. They would hope that by their making such allegations, prisoners might be persuaded to confess to lesser misdeeds.

Five people in my cell, including me, were taken for interrogation on a Monday. On Thursday, we were all brought back but only four of us were left. One of us had been killed under torture. He was accused of belonging to the Mojahedine. Two days later an official newspaper stated that he had been executed but in fact he had died under torture. I witnessed two other cases of death on the torture bed.

In November the court was convened. I was found not guilty but not released. This court told me the young people could smell that I was a counter-revolutionary so I had to stay in prison. The court sat on the fourth floor of the administration building. There are 10 to a dozen courts on the fourth floor of the administration building. The defendants wait outside in a corridor. They are blindfold and taken into the courtroom singly. Usually only the mullah is present. Sometimes there are two people. Sometimes your interrogator is summoned but not as a rule. The mullah says, "Are you wretched?" He asks, "Are you married?" "Do you repent?" and questions like that. It all usually lasts half to one minute which usually gives the mullah a chance to see the man he is to sentence. In Evin they are apt to take pictures of prisoners, especially of any not previously accused. They stick these pictures in albums and show them to other prisoners, particularly collaborators, in order to try and find out more information about them.

An interrogator accused me of having had sexual relations with a woman I knew. This interrogation lasted for two weeks in March 1982. This was during my toughest time in prison. It took me two months to recover.

I did not confess to having had sexual relations with the woman. They inflicted the same tortures as before but more intensively. Being thirsty, I asked for water. They gave me a glass full of urine which I only discovered when I had taken a mouthful. When I put the glass aside, the urine was poured over my head. Pliers were applied to my fingers. In the course of 14 days, I underwent mock execution. The procedure was first of all to be told to write your will. I was told that the religious authorities had condemned me for opposing Islam. I was taken to a place of execution and blindfolded. Then the executioner fired into the air. I was told I had 24 hours in which to confess.

When in April I was brought to court, the hearing lasted no more than a minute. The mullah explained to me that the young people's sense of smell had been correct and advised me to confess so that I could be released. After two weeks I was told my sentence. It was two years. I was taken to Qezel-Hesar Prison in Karaj. I was in Qezel-Hesar until June 1983 when I went back to Evin as there were more accusations. I underwent further interrogations during June. I had again been recognized from pictures. I was accused of being a member of another political organization and a man claimed to know me and said I was one of the top cadres.

I was taken to Block 209 of Evin prison and put in a single cell. Interrogation took place in front of the cells. I was accused of being a leader of the organization. As it was during Ramadan I was able to get some rest at night when the torturers went off to eat. I denied the accusations and after 12 days they seemed to believe me. I was then taken back to court. In court the mullah decided to make a video of me talking about my activities which should later be shown in all the prisons in Iran. I was told that if there were any more allegations against me I would be executed. The video was made, then I waited in my cell for three months. I was summoned to court again in March 1984. I was not called into the courtroom but after waiting outside was told I was free.

——————————Testimony——————————

A teacher, this young man was arrested and tortured several times. Despite his own sufferings, however, he was more affected by the treatment of fellow prisoners, and especially that of his 14-year-old brother who was also held in Tabriz prison. Witnessing the ill-treatment of his brother he described as "the greatest mental torture".

I was first arrested by Revolutionary Guards in January 1980 together with my younger brother who is now a fugitive. I was transferred to a prison run by Revolutionary Guards which had the worst possible conditions — in my cell were just two sponge mattresses, a primus stove heater, and the stinking smell of the toilet which was opposite. Midnight interrogations and mental and physical tortures were the other prevailing conditions which I suffered. After two months, I was released on bail and returned to my work. My brother was released after three months.

In June 1981 I was arrested in my own home town by Revolutionary Guards from Tabriz who took me to Tabriz the same night. This time my 14-year-old brother, who had accompanied the guards to show them where I was staying that night, was also jailed with me.

Before taking me to Tabriz, at the headquarters of Revolutionary Guards in my town, they tied my hands behind my back so tight that I felt my blood-vessels were bursting. They also blindfolded me and put a big paper bag over my head as a sign of contempt. They took off my jacket and threw it over my head and then left me in a yard where there were many other prisoners. There, one of the guards kicked my ankle so hard that I felt pain throughout my body. Inside the minibus carrying us to the prison I moved a little to relax my shoulder muscles. Immediately, one of the guards hit me on the head with a gun-barrel, leaving me motionless. The scar from that blow is still there.

After a few hours' journey, we finally arrived at the prison of the Tabriz Revolutionary Guards. They removed my blindfold to identify me. It was then that I saw my brother and a number of my fellow townsmen. After searching my pockets, the Commander of the guards found my monthly wages, a small sum of money, and said to me: "You have received this money from the *Peykar* Organization." This was their charge against me. As I protested against this baseless accusation, he ordered them to take me to a solitary cell. This measured about 1 metre by 2 metres, with a damp and blood-stained wall behind me, a worn out shabby blanket under me, a steel door, a very strong light which was on all the time, a plastic cup, and a pack of milk on which was written "Produce of Tabriz". Here, I realized that I was in Tabriz. There was no other clue to where I was. The interrogation chamber was next to my room. The sounds of beatings, torture, and threats were the only sounds one could hear.

Once, I wanted to go to the toilet. I still don't know whether it was day or night, because prisoners lose track of time. I knocked on the door and a guard came and started beating and kicking me. After a good beating, he locked the door and left. After a while, I was forced to urinate in the cup. For almost four days they gave me no food or anything else, and my stomach started bleeding. After this, a guard opened the door to give me food. He asked what was in the cup and I told him. Then he told me to drink it. When I refused, he attacked me with a whip and kicked me so much that I was forced to drink it. Then he took me to the toilet and gave me some food and poured me tea in the same cup and said: "Drink it", and when I drank it he left.

The following day they took me to the interrogation chamber. One of the guards asked me to repent and to tell them everything and to divulge my friends' names and promised that they would release me. I said: "I don't know anything, I have nothing to tell you." One of them said: "We shall waste (that is, fire) 20 bullets at you and if you don't tell us the truth, we shall kill you." Then they asked me to make my will to my family. I wrote a letter to my mother. After a few more questions, one of them said: "He is lying about everything. Take him to the basement and give him 80 lashes of the whip and kill him."

They tied my hands and blindfolded me and took me to the basement which was known as "horrific". There, they tied my legs with a long rope. One of them pulled the other end of the rope suddenly and I lost my balance and fell. They started beating me. The scars from that beating are still visible on my back. Then they dragged me near the wall and the Commander of the guards said: "Fire!" I realized later that it was a mock execution, which was far worse than real execution. Amid my screams they fired four bullets at me and then the Commander shouted: "Bring that communist and infidel to be flogged first." They laid me prone on a bed and fastened me to it and started flogging me. After several lashes, they started hitting the soles of my feet with something like a metal bar. I felt as if my bones were melting and then they flogged my back again. I could count up to 56 lashes and heard the guards themselves counting. With every lash they chanted: "*Allah-o-Akbar*" [God is great]. They were laughing at my pain and swearing at me. During the flogging, when I said: "I have backache", one of them stepped on my back and twisted the heel of his boot on my backbone. I fainted.

When I regained consciousness, I found myself between two guards who were holding my arms and asking me to walk. They brought me a big cup of hot tea and said: "Drink, otherwise you die." After a while, they took me to a cell which measured $2\frac{1}{2}$ metres by 3 metres and there were 13 of us in that cell. There was neither a mattress nor anything else, only two or three shabby pieces of sponge which we used as pillows.

After about two months they took us, blindfolded and handcuffed, back to the main prison in Tabriz which was run by the *Komiteh* [the Revolutionary Committee]. They took our clothes and gave me a filthy uniform which was the prison's special uniform. They left me and my brother in a cell in which there were five other prisoners. This place was called Ward 7 or Temporary Ward and usually prisoners who were condemned to death were kept there for a few hours or a few days. Here, our cell was about 1 metre by $1\frac{1}{2}$ metres and the height of its ceiling made it look like a well or a valley of death. It had an uneven concrete floor and a shabby blanket was spread on the floor. Food was given in one dish without any spoon or fork. Each cell was given a loaf of bread. We could go to the toilet only three times a day. The Governor of the prison called at the prison once a month and after picking a few prisoners sent them to another place. Here, they lined up prisoners and he came to know them while asking them questions, whipping and slapping them. One day, he slapped my brother so hard that he fell and I felt the greatest mental torture then. He also flogged my feet and shoulders. After a while, they transferred us to the main hall where there were 1400 prisoners. Because there were no beds, we used to sleep in the corridor on a piece of coarse carpet. Every seven prisoners were given a blanket to share and we used our plastic slippers as our pillows. I slept 116 days on the floor and my backache got worse day by day.

The first time I had a visit from my father was two months after my arrest. At the sight of me, his eyes filled with tears. I had lost 10 kilograms in weight. During other visits in Tabriz Prison we were separated by a screen and could only talk by telephone. These were very short, about two minutes, and sometimes, because the electric current was cut, the visit took place without any conversation.

After seven months, they took me for interrogation. After asking a few questions, the interrogator said to me: "You are lying" and punched me with his fist on my right ear so hard that even now it is not possible for me to hear anything in that ear. He went on flogging and slapping me and then called a guard and said: "Take him to solitary confinement so he can become a human being." I was left, without any covering or anything else, in a small dark room for 24 hours. This room, which was 0.75 metre long and 0.75 metre wide, was like a covered toilet. They kept the prisoner in this place sometimes for several months and gave him his daily dose of flogging. The following day, I was again taken for interrogation. The interrogator, with a kind look, said to me: "Son, I hope you have come to your senses and are not going to torment yourself any more. Tell us everything and save yourself."

My answer, as on the previous occasions, was no. Finally, after further interrogation and punishment, I was returned to my cell. About a week later, by mistake they took my brother — whose name is very similar to mine — to the court instead of me. When the religious judge saw him he said: "In this picture which is in your file, you have a beard and moustache but I see that you are so young that you haven't grown any facial hair." My brother replied: "That is my elder brother." They returned him to his cell. Of the other 13 taken with him to the court, eight were executed and the rest were given life imprisonment or 15 years' imprisonment.

The following day, they took me to the court. The mullah began to read the charges against me, which I had already rejected. Among others, there were 25 charges against me for which, in the opinion of the judge, I had to be executed. However, if I pleaded guilty and repented, he could reduce my punishment. "Printing and distributing leaflets, opposition to and struggle against Imam Khomeini, propagation of communism at school, incitement of students, setting fire to the school, carrying and possessing weapons, taking part in armed clashes..." After reading these charges, he asked me to defend myself. I said: "I do not admit having done any one of those acts. The interrogator has made them up himself. I haven't confessed to doing any one of those." The mullah said: "Here, we have a witness as well who knows you." I asked them to bring their witness to the court. The mullah said: "You and your family are all communists."

After I returned to my cell, he first condemned me to life imprisonment, but later changed his mind and sentenced me to 15 years' imprisonment. My relatives outside the prison were writing letters to the authorities and protesting. They reduced the period of imprisonment first to five years and then to 18 months. Finally, because of my insistence, they brought their witness who said that he didn't know me and had mistaken me for my brother.

I returned to the cell again. It was in the month of Ramadan and I had just gone to sleep, after I had been woken up for the compulsory act of worship, when I was woken up again and taken to the court. My friends were anxious that something might happen to me. I was delivered to another interrogator who was more dangerous than the first. After a short interrogation, he put a paper in front of me and asked me to sign it. When I asked why he replied: "We want to send you to (Ayatollah) Beheshti." (He had been killed that month.) "We want to hang you," he said. I didn't lose my composure and said: "I am innocent, and the execution of an innocent person will be a stain on the reputation of the judiciary." Then, he said: "If we release you, what will you do?" I said: "Looking after my family is my prime duty and I cannot do anything else."

By signing another paper and paying the sum of Rials 200,000 [about £1,770] I was, to my great surprise, released.

About two months after my release from the prison, I was arrested again by the Revolutionary Committee in my own town. They applied the worst tortures to me, including inserting a gun-barrel into my anus; using repulsive language; and concerted kicking and slapping. Then they released me. When they wanted to arrest me again, I fled. When I returned later to the town, I was arrested by Revolutionary Guards. This time, in the Revolutionary Guards prison, they lined us up in a row, blindfolded and with our hands tied, in front of a soccer ball, and then kicked the ball hard at the sensitive parts of our bodies. Once, the ball hit my genitals and as a result of that I urinated blood for some time and every time I was urinating I wished I was dead because of the pain. In one of those nightly interrogations, they punched me on the chin. It took several months for the wound, which was infected, to heal.

These are only some of my memories of the experiences I went through. Even sadder than these are my memories of my fellow prisoners.

Amnesty International —
a worldwide campaign

In recent years, people throughout the world have become more and more aware of the urgent need to protect human rights effectively in every part of the world.

● Countless men and women are in prison for their beliefs. They are being held as prisoners of conscience in scores of countries—in crowded jails, in labour camps and in remote prisons.

● Thousands of political prisoners are being held under administrative detention orders and denied any possibility of a trial or an appeal.

● Others are forcibly confined in psychiatric hospitals or secret detention camps.

● Many are forced to endure relentless, systematic torture.

● More than a hundred countries retain the death penalty.

● Political leaders and ordinary citizens are becoming the victims of abductions, "disappearances" and killings, carried out both by government forces and opposition groups.

An international effort

To end secret arrests, torture and killing requires organized and worldwide effort. Amnesty International is part of that effort.

Launched as an independent organization over 20 years ago, Amnesty International is open to anyone prepared to work universally for the release of prisoners of conscience, for fair trials for political prisoners and for an end to torture and executions.

The movement now has members and supporters in more than 160 countries. It is independent of any government, political group, ideology, economic interest or religious creed.

It began with a newspaper article, "The Forgotten Prisoners", published on 28 May 1961 in *The Observer* (London) and reported in *Le Monde* (Paris).

Announcing an impartial campaign to help victims of political persecution, the British lawyer Peter Benenson wrote:

Open your newspaper any day of the week and you will
find a report from somewhere in the world of someone
being imprisoned, tortured or executed because his opinions
or religion are unacceptable to his government. . . . The
newspaper reader feels a sickening sense of impotence. Yet
if these feelings of disgust all over the world could be
united into common action, something effective could be
done.

Within a week he had received more than a thousand offers of
support—to collect information, publicize it and approach governments. The groundwork was laid for a permanent human rights
organization that eventually became known as Amnesty International. The first chairperson of its International Executive Committee (from 1963 to 1974) was Sean MacBride, who received the
Nobel Peace Prize in 1974 and the Lenin Prize in 1975.

The mandate

Amnesty International is playing a specific role in the international
protection of human rights.

It seeks the *release* of men and women detained anywhere
because of their beliefs, colour, sex, ethnic origin, language
or religious creed, provided they have not used or advocated
violence. These are termed *prisoners of conscience*.

It works for *fair and prompt trials* for *all political prisoners*
and works on behalf of such people detained without charge
or trial.

It opposes the *death penalty* and *torture* or other cruel,
inhuman or degrading treatment or punishment of *all prisoners*
without reservation.

Amnesty International acts on the basis of the Universal Declaration of Human Rights and other international convenants. Amnesty
International is convinced of the indivisibility and mutual depend-
ence of all human rights. Through the practical work for prisoners
within its mandate, Amnesty International participates in the wider
promotion and protection of human rights in the civil, political,
economic, social and cultural spheres.

Amnesty International does not oppose or support any government or political system. Its members around the world include
supporters of differing systems who agree on the defence of all
people in all countries against imprisonment for their beliefs, and
against torture and execution.

Amnesty International at work

The working methods of Amnesty International are based on the principle of international responsibility for the protection of human rights. The movement tries to take action wherever and whenever there are violations of those human rights falling within its mandate. Since it was founded, Amnesty International groups have intervened on behalf of more than 25,000 prisoners in over a hundred countries with widely differing ideologies.

A unique aspect of the work of Amnesty International groups—placing the emphasis on the need for *international* human rights work—is the fact that each group works on behalf of prisoners held in countries other than its own. At least two prisoner cases are assigned to each group; the cases are balanced geographically and politically to ensure impartiality.

There are now 3,341 local Amnesty International groups throughout the world. There are sections in 43 countries (in Africa, Asia, the Americas, Europe and the Middle East) and individual members, subscribers and supporters in more than 120 other countries. Members do not work on cases in their own countries. No section, group or member is expected to provide information on their own country and no section, group or member has any responsibility for action taken or statements issued by the international organization concerning their own country.

Continuous research

The movement attaches the highest importance to balanced and accurate reporting of facts. All its activities depend on meticulous research into allegations of human rights violations. The International Secretariat in London (with a staff of 175, comprising 30 nationalities) has a Research Department which collects and analyses information from a wide variety of sources. These include hundreds of newspapers and journals, government bulletins, transcriptions of radio broadcasts, reports from lawyers and humanitarian organizations, as well as letters from prisoners and their families. Amnesty International also sends fact-finding missions for on-the-spot investigations and to observe trials, meet prisoners and interview government officials. Amnesty International takes full responsibility for its published reports and if proved wrong on any point is prepared to issue a correction.

Once the relevant facts are established, information is sent to sections and groups for action. The members then start the work of trying to protect the individuals whose human rights are reported to have been violated. They send letters to government ministers and embassies. They organize public meetings, arrange special publicity events, such as vigils at appropriate government offices or embassies, and try to interest newspapers in the cases they have taken up. They ask their friends and colleagues to help in the effort. They collect signatures for international petitions and raise money to send relief, such as medicine, food and clothing, to the prisoners and their families.

A permanent campaign

In addition to case work on behalf of individual prisoners, Amnesty International members campaign for the abolition of torture and the death penalty. This includes trying to prevent torture and executions when people have been taken to known torture centres or sentenced to death. Volunteers in dozens of countries can be alerted in such cases, and within hours hundreds of telegrams and other appeals can be on their way to the government, prison or detention centre.

Symbol of
Amnesty International

Amnesty International condemns as a matter of principle the torture and execution of prisoners by *anyone*, including opposition groups. Governments have the responsibility of dealing with such abuses, acting in conformity with international standards for the protection of human rights.

In its efforts to mobilize world public opinion, Amnesty International neither supports nor opposes economic or cultural boycotts. It *does* take a stand against the international transfer of military, police or security equipment and expertise likely to be used by recipient governments to detain prisoners of conscience and to inflict torture and carry out executions.

Amnesty International does not grade governments or countries according to their record on human rights. Not only does repression in various countries prevent the free flow of information about human rights abuses, but the techniques of repression and their impact vary widely. Instead of attempting comparisons, Amnesty International concentrates on trying to end the specific violations of human rights in each case.

Policy and funds

Amnesty International is a democratically run movement. Every two years major policy decisions are taken by an International Council comprising representatives from all the sections. They elect an International Executive Committee to carry out their decisions and supervise the day-to-day running of the International Secretariat.

The organization is financed by its members throughout the world, by individual subscriptions and donations. Members pay fees and conduct fund-raising campaigns—they organize concerts and art auctions and are often to be seen on fund-raising drives at street corners in their neighbourhoods.

Its rules about accepting donations are strict and ensure that any funds received by any part of the organization do not compromise it in any way, affect its integrity, make it dependent on any donor, or limit its freedom of activity.

The organization's accounts are audited annually and are published with its annual report.

Amnesty International has formal relations with the United Nations (ECOSOC), UNESCO, the Council of Europe, the Organization of African Unity and the Organization of American States.